IRON MAIDEN
SONG BY SONG

IRON MAIDEN
SONG BY SONG

CHRISTER BAKKE ANDRESEN

FONTHILL

First published in Great Britain in 2025 by
Fonthill
An imprint of
Pen & Sword Books Ltd
Yorkshire – Philadelphia

Copyright © Christer Bakke Andresen 2025

ISBN 978-1-78155-939-0

The right of Christer Bakke Andresen to be identified as
Author of this work has been asserted by him in accordance
with the Copyright, Designs and Patents Act 1988.

A CIP catalogue record for this book is available from the British Library.

All rights reserved. No part of this book may be reproduced, transmitted, downloaded, decompiled or reverse engineered in any form or by any means, electronic or mechanical including photocopying, recording or by any information storage and retrieval system, without permission from the Publisher in writing. NO AI TRAINING: Without in any way limiting the Author's and Publisher's exclusive rights under copyright, any use of this publication to 'train' generative artificial intelligence (AI) technologies to generate text is expressly prohibited. The Author and Publisher reserve all rights to license uses of this work for generative AI training and development of machine learning language models.

Typeset in Sabon LT Std 10/13
Printed and bound in the UK by CPI Group (UK) Ltd, Croydon, CR0 4YY

The Publisher's authorised representative in the EU for product
safety is Authorised Rep Compliance Ltd., Ground Floor,
71 Lower Baggot Street, Dublin D02 P593, Ireland.
www.arccompliance.com

For a complete list of Pen & Sword titles please contact

PEN & SWORD BOOKS LIMITED
47 Church Street, Barnsley, South Yorkshire, S70 2AS, England
E-mail: enquiries@pen-and-sword.co.uk
Website: www.pen-and-sword.co.uk

Or

PEN AND SWORD BOOKS
1950 Lawrence Rd, Havertown, PA 19083, USA
E-mail: Uspen-and-sword@casematepublishers.com
Website: www.penandswordbooks.com

Preface

Steve Harris once said that his dream was for his band Iron Maiden to record and release fifteen studio albums. In September 2021, Maiden released *Senjutsu*, their seventeenth studio record in a career that now spans five decades. The incredible longevity and influence of Steve Harris' life's work can be appreciated through their albums of music divided into distinctive eras: rising to prominence in the 1980s, struggling through challenging times of upheaval in the 1990s, and then regaining and expanding their prime status in the 2000s and beyond.

Bassist and songwriter Steve Harris stopped playing in other people's bands in 1975, and by Christmas Day that year he had officially assembled the first line-up of his own band, Iron Maiden. Many singers, guitarists and drummers would pass through the revolving door that was the early incarnations of the London-based Maiden, but eventually Harris would decide to build the band around guitarist Dave Murray and drummer Doug Sampson. When this three-piece band found singer Paul Di'Anno in late 1978, the sound of what we know today as the early Iron Maiden was taking shape. The band had garnered a loyal following in the years from 1976 to 1978, and they had already become a popular East London live band by the point that they started gigging with Di'Anno. Now they were eager to take the next step towards Harris' outlandish goal of those fifteen albums.

On New Year's Eve in 1978 Iron Maiden entered Spaceward Studios in Cambridge, taking advantage of cheap downtime at the studio to record four songs for a demo. What was initially known as the 'Spaceward Demo' featured the tracks 'Prowler', 'Invasion', 'Strange World' and 'Iron Maiden'. Maiden handed their demo to DJ Neal Kay at a club called the Bandwagon Heavy Metal Soundhouse in Northwest London, and 'Prowler' would soon become the number one requested song on Kay's club nights. This turned into a lot of attention when Kay published his Soundhouse charts in the *Sounds* music newspaper, with the relatively unknown Iron Maiden's 'Prowler' in the number one spot.

One of the people that would be attracted to Iron Maiden in 1979 through hearing the 'Spaceward Demo' was manager Rod Smallwood. Shortly after joining up with the Steve Harris crew, Smallwood would arrange and negotiate their first record deal with EMI. As the band got closer to recording their debut album in late 1979, they decided to release the demo as an independent vinyl EP titled *The Soundhouse Tapes*. Omitting the wobbly-sounding 'Strange World', the EP included 'Iron Maiden' on side one, plus 'Invasion' and 'Prowler' on side two. In 1996, both 'Iron Maiden' and 'Strange World' would be included on the limited CD edition of the retrospective collection *Best of the Beast*, while all four tracks would be included on the limited vinyl edition. In a little-known footnote, *The Soundhouse Tapes* was recorded by the Iron Maiden line-up that featured Steve Harris (bass), Dave Murray (guitar), Doug Sampson (drums), Paul Di'Anno (vocals), and short-lived second guitarist Paul Cairns, who would never be officially credited for his appearance.

At the same time as they were getting ready for their debut record, Iron Maiden were also offered a spot on EMI's *Metal for Muthas* compilation album featuring bands associated with the burgeoning New Wave of British Heavy Metal movement. Maiden's manager Smallwood was unsure of the wisdom in letting the band dilute their appeal by appearing on a compilation of questionable merit, but he agreed on the condition that Maiden would have two tracks on the record while every other band had only one, and that 'Sanctuary' would be the first song on the first side. Iron Maiden, who had not yet actually signed their contract with EMI, entered EMI's studio in Manchester Square in London to record 'Sanctuary' and 'Wrathchild' with the help of in-house engineer Neal Harrison. The session took place in late October 1979, and the line-up featured Harris, Murray, Sampson and Di'Anno, plus short-lived second guitarist Tony Parsons (who would be gone before the band signed their EMI paperwork in early December). Along with *The Soundhouse Tapes*, the *Metal for Muthas* tracks are the earliest examples of Iron Maiden on vinyl. When the *Metal for Muthas* album was released in February 1980, it added to the hype about the up-and-coming Iron Maiden and the debut album they were going to release in April that year.

The present book is divided into four parts. Part one discusses the Iron Maiden studio albums of the 1980s song by song, while part two goes album by album and song by song through the 1990s. In part three the focus is on the Maiden albums from 2000 and onward, while part four discusses live albums, compilations, video collections and concert features. A comprehensive discography is included as an appendix at the end of the book. It should also be noted that some of the present work is based on previous Iron Maiden catalogue reviews written for the website *Maiden Revelations*. For further reading on the history of Iron Maiden, I humbly suggest visiting www.maidenrevelations.com where in-depth articles and many other fun bits of discussion about the band can be located.

Christer Andresen
Trondheim, Norway, June 2025

Acknowledgements

Many essential books and articles on Iron Maiden have appeared over the years. At the back of this book, you will find listed the chief sources that have gone into the research for the present work. However, special mention should be made of the coverage given to Iron Maiden and their music throughout their history in *Metal Hammer* and *Kerrang!* magazines, as well as the deep-digging official Maiden reference work by Mick Wall, *Run to the Hills: The Authorised Biography*. These have shaped our understanding of Maiden's history.

There would be no such works, and no book from my hand, without the life's work of Steve Harris. What Harris began in 1975, and has continued to the present day, has given joy and inspiration to millions around the world. Steve Harris and all his comrades through the band's many incarnations have changed lives and rerouted rock history. Personally, I cannot imagine a world without Iron Maiden, and for that I am grateful.

I extend particular gratitude to Torgrim Øyre, without whom there would be no *Maiden Revelations* website and I would not be writing about Iron Maiden today.

Up the Irons!

Contents

Preface   5

Acknowledgements   8

PART ONE: THE 1980s   11

    1   *Iron Maiden*   12

    2   *Killers*   20

    3   *The Number of the Beast*   28

    4   *Piece of Mind*   35

    5   *Powerslave*   41

    6   *Somewhere in Time*   48

    7   *Seventh Son of a Seventh Son*   55

PART TWO: THE 1990s   63

    8   *No Prayer for the Dying*   64

    9   *Fear of the Dark*   70

    10   *The X Factor*   78

    11   *Virtual XI*   86

Part Three: The 2000s and Beyond — 93

12 *Brave New World* — 94
13 *Dance of Death* — 101
14 *A Matter of Life and Death* — 107
15 *The Final Frontier* — 112
16 *The Book of Souls* — 118
17 *Senjutsu* — 123

Part Four: Other Recordings — 129

18 Live Albums — 130
19 Compilations — 139
20 Video Albums — 142

Discography — 147

Sources — 152

PART ONE

The 1980s

1

Iron Maiden

Produced by Will Malone
Released 14 April 1980
Highest chart position and certification at 4/Platinum (UK), –/Gold (US)
Featuring Steve Harris (bass), Dave Murray (guitar), Paul Di'Anno (vocals), Dennis Stratton (guitar), Clive Burr (drums)

Although the band (and Steve Harris in particular) have always been critical of the primitive Will Malone production for the *Iron Maiden* album, the energy and momentum of Iron Maiden in full flight is immediately apparent. It certainly sounds raw and unpolished, brittle guitars and cardboard drums included, and yet this seems the right sound for Maiden's debut in retrospect. There would be giant sonic leaps to make from here as the band moved on to subsequent records, but musically speaking they already had the goods.

Iron Maiden was recorded at Kingsway Studios in London, England in January 1980 and mixed at Morgan Studios in February. Andy Scott, guitarist in The Sweet, had been suggested as producer but rejected by Steve Harris, and Maiden ended up working with Will Malone. In truth, Malone might not have been enthusiastic about producing this unknown band, but engineer Martin Levan, who would go on to have a distinguished career in musicals where he worked regularly with Andrew Lloyd Webber, helped them achieve a fair working environment in the studio. The album was recorded by a very fresh line-up, guitarist Dennis Stratton and drummer Clive Burr both having joined Maiden in December 1979.

The resulting record might not have sounded the way Steve Harris had hoped, but it gave Iron Maiden a first and unexpected hit when it reached number 4 in the UK album chart on its release. At this point Maiden were seen as a leading light in the so-called New Wave of British Heavy Metal movement, along with bands like Def Leppard, Diamond Head and Venom, and many reviewers hailed their debut record as a breath of fresh air that broke new ground for heavy metal music going into the 1980s. It seems clear that the lack of production value on *Iron Maiden* was not held against it, and it could be argued that the primitive sound of the album coupled with the down-to-earth quality of the band themselves resonated with the punk-driven reaction against pompous 1970s hard rock at the time.

While the band recorded, manager Rod Smallwood had gone hunting for the proper cover art, since no one wanted to have the band on the album cover. What he found was the twisted image of a character to become known as Eddie, created by artist Derek Riggs. The original Riggs illustration was revised on Smallwood's instructions and turned into the *Iron Maiden* cover image that effectively started Eddie off on a surreal journey from city streets to ethereal realms that would accompany the Maiden music throughout the 1980s.

'Prowler'

The timeless 'Prowler' opens the album in excellent style. Originally presented on *The Soundhouse Tapes*, this early 1980 re-recording sounds better. Dennis Stratton's one-chord riff is joined by Dave Murray's sweet melody before the whole band kicks in. The balance of tone provided by the clash of Murray's 1957 Fender Stratocaster with Stratton's Gibson Les Paul is a cornerstone of the early Maiden sound that would be further developed when Adrian Smith joined the band in Stratton's place. It also sounds like Steve Harris and Clive Burr have played together for much longer than just a few weeks, the rhythm section backing the song up in a very tight and precise manner. Over the top of it all comes Paul Di'Anno with his trademark gruffy vocals, perfectly embodying the voice of Maiden for all who discovered them at that early time in their career.

'Prowler' was written by Steve Harris, and it shows off both harmony vocals and harmony guitars in a way that is tastefully restrained and points ahead to decades of Iron Maiden music to come. Another Harris hallmark is the unexpected song structure where a breakdown and a tempo change come in following the first chorus. The song then heads into a blistering guitar solo and another chorus in the same high tempo, before slowing back down to its original pace for another verse and chorus. Conventional it is certainly not.

'Remember Tomorrow'

With music by Harris and lyrics from Di'Anno, 'Remember Tomorrow' is the original quiet-beginning-erupting-into-metal-fury Iron Maiden track. The band would do a lot of these throughout their career, and they can all be traced back to this otherworldly song that was reportedly inspired by the slow passing of Di'Anno's grandfather.

Indeed, the lyrics are an interesting point of study on the *Iron Maiden* album. Whereas the opener 'Prowler' had talked about showing off private parts to unsuspecting girls while 'crawling through the bushes', and the later 'Running Free' would discuss the pulling of birds, the driving of pick-up trucks, and spending nights in jail, there is a telling contrast in the introspective and pondering lyrics for 'Remember Tomorrow' that points ahead to the more serious and mature directions that Maiden's lyrics would take on albums to come: 'Unchain the colours before my eyes / Yesterday's sorrows, tomorrow's white lies.'

'Running Free'

In a case of light following shade comes the surprisingly simplistic and catchy 'Running Free'. The band is on fire, their punkish energy balanced by first-class musicianship. Di'Anno wails, shouts, and grunts his way through the lyrics, Harris' bass gels perfectly with Burr's energetic drumming, and the guitar team of Murray and Stratton sound on top shredder form throughout the barrage of riffs, power chords and harmonies.

In fact, 'Running Free' cracked the Top 40 in Great Britain when it was released as a single. To the lasting shock of the people at EMI, Iron Maiden were invited to play on *Top of the Pops*, where they were even allowed to perform live. Maiden had certainly built a strong following for themselves by that point, but the effect of being exposed on national television on the eve of their first album's release should not be underestimated. The songwriting clash of Harris and Di'Anno had resulted in the perfect track for this occasion.

The 'Running Free' single preceded the *Iron Maiden* album in February 1980. This single release would therefore also provide the public with their first glimpse of Derek Riggs' Eddie, a threatening figure chasing a young man through a dark alley. Eddie is wielding a broken bottle, but his face is obscured by shadow in anticipation of the album's reveal.

'Phantom of the Opera'

If the horrific aesthetics of Eddie were already apparent, a similar motif of horror and fantasy would soon become detectable in Iron Maiden's music and lyrics too. Steve Harris' breakthrough composition 'Phantom of the Opera' is the first of many overtly horror-themed Maiden tunes to come, probably inspired by film adaptations of the 1909 Gaston Leroux novel.

The first in Harris' long line of storytelling epics through the decades, the theatrical drama of the source material is a perfect match for his inventive musical passages, bringing the listener into the darkness of the theatre: 'You're standing in the wings / There you wait for the curtain to fall.'

'Phantom of the Opera' is truly the song where the unconventional style of Harris' songwriting came to the forefront. Probably owing something to his love of progressive rock artists like Jethro Tull and Genesis, Harris seems completely uninterested in traditional rock song formats and approaches 'Phantom of the Opera' more like a film score. There is no calculated sequence of verse-chorus-verse-chorus-bridge-chorus anywhere in sight. The band ebbs and flows through a tasteful selection of compositions that are somehow seamlessly stitched together into a whole, and it seems the most natural thing in the world of music. The frantic shuffle of the opening verses morphs into a rhythmic stomp that in turn gives way to a quiet section for Murray to solo over, and then comes the bass arpeggios that lead into the galloping groove over which Murray and Stratton weave one of Maiden's signature minor third harmony runs. Back into the frantic shuffle riffing, the story concludes with the lament that 'You damaged my mind / And my soul it just floats through the air.' Steve Harris himself would later recall the track as a turning point for his songwriting and his band, saying that it made him see clearer where he wanted to take things in the years to come.

'TRANSYLVANIA'

The horror motif extends to the title of the instrumental 'Transylvania', which is the home of Dracula, of course. The songs on *Iron Maiden* are essentially selected snapshots from the band's early live shows, and 'Transylvania', written by Steve Harris, was an effective track to get the audience on their feet. It feels like a natural extension from 'Phantom of the Opera', and as such it makes the flow of the album seem effortless. There were other tracks available with lyrics and vocals, some of which would show up on the next record, but the presence of 'Transylvania' suggests that the band wanted an instrumental on the album and that this one was popular with their audience at the time. In later years it would sometimes function as an intro piece played over the PA prior to Iron Maiden taking the stage, and it was also played live by the band on the 1993 *Real Live Tour* in Europe.

'STRANGE WORLD'

Here is a one-off in the Iron Maiden canon. The band would never again record a song that sounds anything like 'Strange World', which most of all seems to be Maiden's take on a Jimi Hendrix-style ballad. Originally presented on *The Soundhouse Tapes* in 1979, it was re-recorded for the *Iron Maiden* album. Once again written by Steve Harris, this song is another example of the diversity that makes *Iron Maiden* stand out as a debut record. Paul Di'Anno has never sounded as unaffected as he does on this recording of 'Strange World'. Projecting the song's ethereal lyrics about 'ship of white light in the sky' and 'stalks of light come from the ground', the singer reaches a career high, supported by tasteful guitar work from Murray and Stratton, while Harris and Burr recede into the background in an impressively mature understanding of performance dynamics. Along with 'Remember Tomorrow' this song stands out as a counterpoint to the fury with which the band attacks most of their songs.

'CHARLOTTE THE HARLOT'
In stark contrast to the preceding track, 'Charlotte the Harlot' dispenses with any subtlety. Discussing the life of a London prostitute, somewhat hypocritically denouncing her for her immoral occupation, this is the only track on the album credited to guitarist Dave Murray. While he could certainly write the music, he has never been known as a lyricist. It is quite possible that Steve Harris wrote the lyrics, but they have also been claimed by previous singer Dennis Wilcock (who sang with the band from 1976 to 1978). The issue of former band members having some uncredited stake in the songs on the first two Iron Maiden albums has been debated in later years, and 'Charlotte the Harlot' bearing the lone Murray credit frankly defies probability.

Musically the song is built to show off Murray's effortless riffing, as well as his sensitive solo work in the quiet middle section. Along with 'Strange World' this is a track from the *Iron Maiden* album that would disappear from concert setlists during the *Killers* tour in 1981. They did give 'Charlotte the Harlot' a go at the very beginning of their *Early Days* tour in 2005 (performing songs from only their first four records), but it was quickly replaced by the presumably more audience friendly 'Wrathchild' from *Killers*. Besides the upcoming title track, 'Running Free' is the most frequently performed song from this album, followed by 'Phantom of the Opera'. The 2005 tour saw the live reappearances of 'Prowler' and 'Remember Tomorrow', probably for the final time.

'IRON MAIDEN'
Then, of course, there is 'Iron Maiden', the perennial main set-closer where Eddie makes his most stage-encompassing appearance to bring the house down. In truth it is one of the most primitive songs on the *Iron Maiden* album, and it is very unlikely to have become a concert regular throughout all their history without the Eddie theatrics linked with it. The song was originally presented on *The Soundhouse Tapes* and then re-recorded for this album.

'Iron Maiden' is credited to Steve Harris only, but like the previous track 'Charlotte the Harlot' it seems to have a more tangled creation history. Even the official Maiden biography by journalist and author Mick Wall gives room to former guitarist Dave Sullivan, who claims to have come up with the song's opening riff. That riff would be turned into the two-guitar harmony part that was so essential to Harris' musical ideal at the time, leading into the simple two-chord verse and the slightly poppy major-key chorus about Iron Maiden coming to get you, wherever you are.

The lyrics seem to discuss something to do with the medieval torture device that lends its name to the band, the song, and the album, and so 'Iron Maiden' completes the horror cycle that started with 'Phantom of the Opera' and continued with 'Transylvania', a motif that would come to its fullest expression on the band's next album, *Killers*.

RELATED RECORDINGS

Several other recordings were made around the same time as the *Iron Maiden* album, and they flesh out the early history of the band. After making their vinyl debut with the independent *The Soundhouse Tapes* EP in 1979, then teasing their audience with their two tracks on *Metal for Muthas* in early 1980 before finally launching their first record, it seems that Iron Maiden were intent on cleaning house before recording their second album.

'Sanctuary' was originally recorded in late October 1979 at EMI's Manchester Square studio in London with in-house engineer Neal Harrison, and subsequently released on the *Metal for Muthas* compilation in February 1980 along with 'Wrathchild' from the same recording session. 'Sanctuary' was then re-recorded and released as a non-album single in May 1980. This version, credited to producer Will Malone but sounding like a different recording project than the *Iron Maiden* album proper, was added to the North American edition of *Iron Maiden* released by Capitol EMI in the summer of 1980, where it was put between 'Strange World' and 'Charlotte the Harlot.' The track was later also added to the 1998 CD remaster where it followed 'Prowler' at the start of the album, and then removed again from the later vinyl reissues and the 2015 digital remaster and current CD edition. 'Sanctuary' was originally credited only to Steve Harris on *Metal for Muthas*, and later bore the deceptive credit Iron Maiden, as in the whole band. But there is some evidence that former guitarist Bob Sawyer (later known as Rob Angelo), who was in the band for a short time in 1977, co-wrote the track and was paid to give up his credit. In later years the song has been re-credited to Murray, Harris and Di'Anno, as Maiden have persisted in not crediting any pre-1980 members. The Derek Riggs artwork for the single cover depicts Eddie crouching over the dead body of Prime Minister Margaret Thatcher, a provocation that triggered the desired conservative outrage and gave Maiden some media attention.

'Burning Ambition', possibly the first song that Steve Harris ever wrote, is the only known track from a studio exploration with producer Gary Edwards in late November 1979, sandwiched between the *Metal for Muthas* recording in October and the sessions for the band's debut album that would take place in January 1980. This song was recorded as a four-piece band with Dave Murray performing all the guitar parts, as second guitarist Tony Parsons had been let go from the band shortly after they performed at the *BBC* Friday Rock Show on radio on 14 November. The 'Burning Ambition' track was released as the B-side to the 'Running Free' single in February 1980 and features Doug Sampson on the drums, not long before his replacement by Clive Burr in December 1979.

'Women in Uniform' was recorded in the summer of 1980 in London's Battery Studios (which Maiden would utilise for their next two album projects) and released in October that year as a non-album single. The song is a cover of the 1978 hit by the Australian band Skyhooks, and it was suggested to Maiden by their publishing company Zomba, along with producer Tony Platt. The idea might have been to establish a commercial collaboration with a view to the next Iron Maiden album, but it backfired badly when Steve Harris fell out with Platt over production issues and the way the producer tried to steer Maiden in a poppier direction. This is the last recording to feature guitarist Dennis Stratton, as he would be replaced by Adrian Smith shortly following the 'Women in Uniform' video shoot at London's Rainbow Theatre in October 1980. The Derek Riggs artwork for the single cover depicts Margaret Thatcher (alive again, and inevitably in uniform) about to have her violent revenge on Eddie, and it was clear that the tradition of great Iron Maiden packaging, and the effort to tell stories with album and single artworks, was already being established.

'Invasion', another early Steve Harris composition, first appeared on *The Soundhouse Tapes* in 1979, and it was later re-recorded at the 'Women in Uniform' sessions with Tony Platt in the summer of 1980. The song was released as the B-side to the 'Women in Uniform' single.

December 1980 saw the Japan-only release of the EP 'Live!! +one'. The plus one track was the recently released single 'Women in Uniform', while the other tracks were recorded live at London's Marquee Club on 4 July 1980 by front-of-house engineer Doug Hall. Of these, 'Sanctuary' and 'Drifter' are exclusive to the 'Live!! +one' release, while 'Phantom of the Opera' was also issued as a second B-side to the 'Women in Uniform' single. 'Live!! +one' would be reissued in Greece in 1984, with an expanded track listing that included the Montrose cover 'I've Got the Fire' recorded at the Marquee on 3 April 1980 as well as the live tracks featured on the *Maiden Japan* EP that was released in 1981 at the end of Maiden's *Killers* cycle.

In 1995 *Iron Maiden* was reissued on CD with a bonus disc that featured both 'Sanctuary' and 'Burning Ambition' along with live recordings of the

Killers track 'Drifter' and the Montrose song 'I've Got the Fire'. The latter two were recorded at Maiden's 3 April 1980 concert at London's Marquee Club and had been featured as B-side tracks on the 'Sanctuary' single in May 1980. The 'Women in Uniform' single track and its B-sides 'Invasion' and 'Phantom of the Opera (live)' would somewhat confusingly appear on the bonus disc to the 1995 CD reissue of *Killers*, probably because the 'Women in Uniform' release in late 1980 was very close to the *Killers* release in early 1981 that the band were gearing up for at the time, plus the fact that 'Women in Uniform' had been included on the Australian edition of *Killers*.

Listening preferences

The Iron Maiden catalogue was remastered for CD in 1998, up to and including 1992's *Fear of the Dark* album. These reissues were unfortunate examples of the loudness war of the late 1990s and early 2000s, so called because mastering of music recordings for CD had become a battle to push all frequencies to their highest possible level, partially through dynamic range compression, leaving little room for dynamics and inducing listening fatigue. Preferences will ever be subjective, of course, but many Maiden fans and connoisseurs would argue that editions either before or after 1998 are clearly preferable to these remasters.

Some would say that the original mix of *Iron Maiden* is simply not good enough to be preferable in any mastering version, but many would prefer the early 1980s vinyl editions or the late 1980s CD editions. The overloud 1998 CD remaster regrettably brings forth the less flattering characteristics of the brittle guitar sound, so the later 2014 vinyl reissue (cut from the original 1980 analogue master) and the 2015 digital remaster which is currently available on CD and streaming services are tangibly more pleasant on the ears. It remains to be seen if Harris and Smallwood will ever want to have *Iron Maiden* remixed for some sort of deluxe edition reissue down the road, a trend that many other artists (including Harris' old favourites Jethro Tull) have successfully embraced in recent years.

2
Killers

Produced by Martin 'Headmaster' Birch
Released 16 February 1981
Highest chart position and certification at 12/gold (UK) and 78/gold (US)
Featuring Steve Harris (bass), Dave Murray (guitar), Paul Di'Anno (vocals), Clive Burr (drums), Adrian Smith (guitar)

After scoring a surprise hit with their debut album *Iron Maiden* in 1980, as well as showcasing themselves in high profile support slots on tours with Judas Priest in the UK and KISS in Europe, Iron Maiden was the up-and-coming band to watch in 1981. Sonically, the *Killers* album is in a different league from the *Iron Maiden* debut. After aborted or disappointing collaborations with Neal Harrison, Gary Edwards, Andy Scott, Will Malone and Tony Platt, Iron Maiden finally found their producer: Martin Birch. Already a rock production legend at that time due to his fine work with Deep Purple and Black Sabbath among others, Birch would prove to be the perfect conduit and engineer for Steve Harris and his struggling band in the early 1980s. *Killers* was recorded and mixed in London's Battery Studios from December 1980 into January 1981, and it was co-engineered by Nigel Green (then known as Nigel Hewitt), who would later work with Iron Maiden in the mid-1990s.

Another crucial step in the development of Iron Maiden at the time of *Killers* was the arrival of guitarist and songwriter Adrian Smith. He had been the first choice for Harris and Murray when they looked for a second guitarist in late 1979, but he had rejected the Maiden offer because his own band Urchin appeared to be taking off at the time. A year later, at the end of 1980, Urchin had failed, and Maiden were about to fire Dennis Stratton. At last, the stars aligned, and the Iron Maiden guitar department got its choice combination: Murray and Smith would from this point on become a leading guitar partnership in the 1980s, Murray's virtuoso fretwork perfectly complemented by Smith's melodic and rhythmic leads.

Very much a companion piece to the first album, *Killers* features several songs that had already been in the Iron Maiden live set for years. Ultimately, the biggest difference between *Killers* and its predecessor is the quality of the production. With Martin Birch at the controls, Maiden could relax and perform. Although the following year's *The Number of the Beast* would forever be regarded as Maiden's breakthrough album, *Killers* is where the quintessential Iron Maiden sound was truly born.

Even so, *Killers* faced a critical backlash in the UK, where some reviews were downright harsh and hostile. The album did not chart as high as Maiden's debut album had done in their home country, but overall the *Killers* album sold better internationally and marked Iron Maiden's first appearance on the US Billboard chart as their first tour of North America in the summer of 1981 paid off in album sales and attention.

Killers is not a concept album, but the title indicates a common theme running through its lyrics: death and dying, murderers and victims, around the world and through the ages. Manager Rod Smallwood commissioned another Derek Riggs painting, and now Eddie came into his own and took on the appearance that fans would forever celebrate as the ultimate incarnation. Wielding a bloody axe, his victim clinging to the front of his shirt, the murderous expression on Eddie's face was the perfect visual to go with the new Maiden music.

'THE IDES OF MARCH'

Killers kicks off with one of the most atmospheric pieces of Maiden music, the instrumental 'The Ides of March.' The title is lifted from the Roman calendar's 15 March, a date of religious observance and the date when Julius Caesar was assassinated in 44 BCE, making it a term for 'turning point' in later ages, and inspiring the Shakespearean warning 'beware the Ides of March.' For Maiden it marks the point when their sound became world-conquering.

The piece is credited to Steve Harris alone, but there is some evidence that former Maiden drummer Barry 'Thunderstick' Purkis could have had a couple of drumsticks in it. Purkis joined Samson after leaving Maiden in 1978, and the same track would feature on their 1980 album *Head On*, with the title 'Thunderburst'. On the Samson album the track is credited to Harris and Purkis along with the rest of Samson. Assuming this is as incorrect as the sole Harris credit on the *Killers* album, it seems a reasonable middle ground to speculate that the bassist and drummer might have cooked up the music in some sort of collaboration.

What truly sets the Maiden version far apart from the Samson version is the delicate atmosphere created by the harmonic interplay and lead trade-offs between Dave Murray and Adrian Smith, signalling clearly that Iron Maiden now had a world-class guitar duo able to conjure up moods and colours for the dramas of their Harris-led compositions.

'WRATHCHILD'

This is a Steve Harris composition that had been in the Iron Maiden live set for years, and it was first presented on the *Metal for Muthas* compilation album in early 1980. However, this re-recording is triumphant proof of how right it was for Maiden to be produced by Martin Birch: Unlike any earlier recording of the band, here is the fat low-end, the hard-hitting drums, the powerful guitars, and the perfectly judged vocal performances, all of which would come to characterise classic era Iron Maiden.

The song was already a live favourite, and in the decades to come 'Wrathchild' would regularly appear in concert as a dependable crowd-pleaser, usually quite early in the set. The groovy bass riff that opens the song is built to get the crowd going, and this *Killers* version of the track is distinguished by the sharing of leads and guitar fills between Murray and Smith. Mention must be made of Clive Burr's drumming, as he effortlessly drives the band onward at a brisker pace than what Doug Sampson had done with the earlier *Metal for Muthas* recording.

'MURDERS IN THE RUE MORGUE'

One of the few tracks on *Killers* that were brand new at the time, 'Murders in the Rue Morgue' takes its title from the 1841 short story by Edgar Allan Poe. Celebrated as one of the first modern detective stories, this is a tale of murder and misfortune in Paris. After a quiet intro featuring a beautiful lead bass melody, the song leaps into a paranoid pace of verses and choruses, tastefully broken up by a dramatic harmony guitar part that leads back into a chorus and another verse and chorus. 'Murders in the Rue Morgue' is in fact one of the more formulaically structured tracks in the early Maiden catalogue.

The song is credited to Steve Harris. However, the official Mick Wall biography of the band states matter-of-factly that Adrian Smith was now on hand to help Maiden knock some new songs into shape, including 'Murders in the Rue Morgue', which raises the question of potential uncredited co-writing. This is particularly relevant because Smith himself has in later years stated that he had a hand in writing the non-album single 'Twilight Zone', for which he is not credited. In what would become a recurring issue with Iron Maiden, members are not credited for songwriting on their first album with the band, even when it is obvious and well known that they did contribute. When it comes to Smith and 'Murders in the Rue Morgue', his involvement remains speculation.

'Another Life'
This is a Harris number going back to at least 1979, like many *Killers* tracks having been a regular in concert setlists for years before its album debut. The rather simplistic chord patterns of the song are thankfully spiced up by very catchy lead guitar work. It is hard to imagine this track working properly on the previous record, without the aid of the dynamic and powerful Martin Birch production to bolster its appeal. A strange feature of 'Another Life' is the fact that it has only one verse of lyrics, and this one verse is repeated three times throughout the song. An added awkwardness comes from the absence of any chorus to resolve the tension set up in the verse. There is an odd and not very Maiden-like sense of resignation and lack of energy in the verse's concluding line 'But I'm so tired of living / I might as well end today'.

'Genghis Khan'
Instrumentals were a common occurrence in the early days of Iron Maiden. The first album had 'Transylvania', while *Killers* opened with 'The Ides of March' and also includes the brand-new Harris composition 'Genghis Khan' for good measure. The track is named after the first Emperor of the expansionist Mongol Empire in the early 1200s, and it is the first example of Maiden being inspired by Middle Eastern music. The opening section of the song resembles a march, befitting the titular historical character's conquering march into China and Central Asia. The middle section then bursts into battle with the intense fury of Burr's drums and the whirlwind riffs of bassist Harris and guitarists Murray and Smith. The final section calms down to a gentle gallop over which is draped a beautiful example of Maiden's minor third guitar harmonies. This section was used as an effective intro to the 1993 *Raising Hell* TV concert, but 'Genghis Khan' would otherwise not survive in the setlist beyond the 1981 *Killers* tour.

'Innocent Exile'
Here is yet another early Maiden number by Harris which had been in the band's setlist for years prior to being recorded for *Killers*. Kicking off with a patented idiosyncratic bass riff, 'Innocent Exile' is another song of death and misery, this time from the point of view of a man wrongfully accused of killing a woman. In a similar vein to 'Wrathchild', 'Innocent Exile' bounces along in a mid-paced gallop, except when it breaks off into a quicker shuffle over which the two guitarists trade solo spots. It is another one of the *Killers* tracks that would forever disappear from the band's setlist after the 1981 *Killer World Tour*.

'KILLERS'

A highlight of the album is the title track. 'Killers' had been in the Iron Maiden live set since the summer of 1980, and would ultimately become a prime example of the power of the Paul Di'Anno era when filtered through the production expertise of Martin Birch. It is astonishing that this recording was made less than a year after the band's first album. The Maiden gallop was becoming a hallmark by this point, and 'Killers' would sound just as impressive when it was performed by the subsequent Bruce Dickinson line-up of the band on the following year's *The Number of the Beast* tour.

The music was written by Harris and the lyrics by Di'Anno. In December 1980 the song had been featured in the concert that was filmed for *Live at the Rainbow*, but even if this was about the same time as the studio sessions for *Killers*, the lyrics at the concert were completely different from the ones (thankfully) re-written for the album. The disturbing words are mostly sung from the point of view of a non-repentant murderer, bringing the album title and cover artwork into chilling perspective.

'PRODIGAL SON'

The lack of repentance in the lyrics to the title track is immediately followed by the ultimate contrast in the album's ballad, 'Prodigal Son' doing for *Killers* what 'Strange World' had done for *Iron Maiden* the year before. The point of view this time is that of someone who prays to the mythical monster Lamia to help release the devil's hold on his soul.

This semi-acoustic song is a stirring example of the musical sophistication that Iron Maiden could exhibit from the very start of their career, but it is the only *Killers* track never to be performed in concert. 'Prodigal Son' is credited to Harris, but it is another one of the late additions to the *Killers* repertoire that Smith helped to 'knock into shape', as the official biography states it. Whether this means co-writing, as was clearly the case with the non-album single 'Twilight Zone', must remain speculation. In any case, Smith's playing is heard and even felt all over this outstanding track.

'PURGATORY'

In the early days of Maiden, possibly as far back as 1976, the band worked on a ballad-like slow number called 'Floating', written by Harris. In the preparation of material for *Killers*, the song was sped up significantly and turned into the riff-fest 'Purgatory'. This is a song that certainly plays to the strengths of the Harris and Burr rhythm section as well as the Murray and Smith guitar pairing, while still leaving enough room for a Di'Anno on top form to deliver one of his most memorable Iron Maiden performances. 'Purgatory' is a deliciously melodic and yet frantically fast-paced piece of heavy metal that sounds unique and fresh even in the present day. With lyrics that seem to discuss an out-of-body or near-death experience, 'Purgatory' was released as the second single from the *Killers* album in June 1981, but it would never return to the band's concert setlist after the 1981 tour.

'Drifter'

Another early Maiden number by Harris, already released as a live version on the 'Sanctuary' single's B-side in 1980, 'Drifter' is characterised by the descending guitar riff that opens the song and repeats throughout. Along with 'Phantom of the Opera' it is also another early example of Harris' fondness for the fast-paced shuffle beat. 'Drifter' used to appear close to the end of Iron Maiden's concerts in the early days (sometimes even as the last song) and would do so up until and including the *Piece of Mind* tour in 1983.

However, with the exception of 'Wrathchild', tracks from this album would rarely appear in setlists after the earliest years of Maiden's recording career. On the retrospective *Early Days* tour in 2005 some of the *Killers* songs would see a return: 'The Ides of March' as a pre-recorded intro, 'Murders in the Rue Morgue' as opener, 'Another Life' and 'Wrathchild' in the main set, and 'Drifter' in the encore. The strange omission on this occasion was the title track, which had previously enjoyed brief comebacks at the end of the 1988 *Seventh Son of a Seventh Son* tour and on the 1999 reunion tour with Bruce Dickinson and Adrian Smith. The lack of *Killers* material in Maiden's concert setlists is perhaps most perplexing because Steve Harris is on record several times stating that he always thought *Killers* was Maiden's strongest album until *Piece of Mind*, which means (strange though it may seem to the more casual follower) that he felt it was stronger than the breakthrough *The Number of the Beast* record that followed it.

Then, as Iron Maiden launched their fiftieth anniversary tour *Run for Your Lives* in 2025, the *Killers* album got its place in the spotlight. The set opened with a generous helping of tracks from the record: 'The Ides of March' once again as a pre-recorded intro, 'Murders in the Rue Morgue' as opener, now also featuring its complete intro unlike in 2005, 'Wrathchild' next, and then 'Killers' with a walk-on Eddie stalking the band around the stage, axe in hand.

Related recordings

A month after the release of *Killers*, Iron Maiden released the first single related to it in March 1981. They decided to do what is weirdly called a double A-side, issuing the non-album track 'Twilight Zone' along with 'Wrathchild'. The thinking might have been that they had a live video of 'Wrathchild' available from filming *Live at the Rainbow* the previous December, a concert video feature that would see release in May 1981.

'Twilight Zone' would subsequently be added to the North American edition of *Killers* in the summer of 1981, appearing between 'Killers' and 'Prodigal Son'. This spot in the track listing would be taken by 'Women in Uniform', a 1980 non-album single, on the Australian edition. 'Twilight Zone' would also appear as the last song on the Japanese edition of the album, as the misprinted 'Details of Twilight Zone'. On the 1998 CD remaster edition of the album, 'Twilight Zone' would appear next-to-last ahead of album closer 'Drifter', while it would be removed again for the current vinyl reissues and the 2015 digital remaster available on CD.

'Twilight Zone' is credited to Dave Murray and Steve Harris, but Adrian Smith has also claimed involvement with the writing of this song. In an *eonmusic* interview in 2020, Smith would state that Harris wasn't around much when the two guitarists finished writing 'Twilight Zone', and that Smith himself wrote all the harmony guitar parts and had a hand in writing the chord progressions as well. This is an interesting case of apparent Maiden politics, pointing back to the exclusion of pre-1980 band members in the songwriting credits and ahead to the absence of credits for Bruce Dickinson and Janick Gers on their respective first albums with the band in 1982 and 1990.

The second *Killers* single consisted of two songs right off the album, the A-side 'Purgatory' and the B-side 'Genghis Khan', and thus held very little interest for anyone who already owned the album. Perhaps the most interesting footnote about this single release is the Derek Riggs cover artwork. The image of the devil shedding his face as a mask that covers Eddie's face was in fact a last-minute replacement. The image that Riggs had originally painted for 'Purgatory' was deemed too good to be wasted on an obscure single and would become the cover artwork for *The Number of the Beast* in 1982.

Apparently, the Japanese arm of Iron Maiden's record company, Toshiba EMI, wanted a live album from the band. Maiden and Smallwood resisted this, but they seem to have allowed for the compromise that was the 'Maiden Japan' live EP. Released in September 1981, just as Iron Maiden were about to replace Paul Di'Anno with Bruce Dickinson, 'Maiden Japan' was recorded in Nagoya in May on the band's first tour of Japan. The Japanese and European edition consisted of the tracks 'Running Free', 'Remember Tomorrow', 'Killers' and 'Innocent Exile', while the so-called international edition also added 'Wrathchild' in the middle of the running order. The EP features a solid mix by front-of-house engineer Doug Hall, and although the entire concert has been bootlegged it is to be hoped that Maiden and Smallwood will find the opportunity to do a *Killers* deluxe edition at some point that features the complete concert recording.

Listening preferences

As stated in the previous chapter, preferences will ever be subjective, but many Maiden fans and connoisseurs would argue that editions either before or after the 1998 CD remasters are preferable, the 1998 editions generally being plagued by the loudness war mastering that sacrificed subtlety and dynamic range in order to impress with pure volume. Depending on the sound system you use, as well as your own preferences, this loudness and compression is either a good or a bad thing. In any case, this mastering issue is less apparent with the 1998 edition of *Killers* than most of the other albums.

Killers sounds excellent in its original 1981 vinyl incarnation, and also in its first appearance on CD, which was the Japanese Toshiba printing in 1986. The 1995 CD reissue featuring a bonus disc of the aforementioned related recordings still sounds good, albeit a little fainter than the previous CD editions, which is a rare criticism when it comes to digital music formats. At the other end of the scale the 1998 CD remaster is louder and audibly compressed, while there has more recently been the 2014 heavyweight vinyl reissue which was cut from the original analogue 1981 master, and the digital remaster from 2015 which is currently available on CD and streaming services. These latest vinyl and CD editions sound good, although quite a bit louder than the 1980s vinyl and CD editions.

For collectors of vintage vinyl, there is another point to be made. Opinions will obviously differ, but to the author's ears it seems that original Japanese pressings of Maiden's 1980s albums sound extraordinarily good. Others will claim, with good reason, that original UK pressings are the best. Ditto for original US pressings. And, more surprisingly, a case can be made for the Russian 1993 reissues by Gala Records.

It should also be noted that all Iron Maiden albums sound good when streamed from a high-quality service through high-quality headphones or speaker systems, although one should be aware that these editions are the 2015 digital remaster.

3

The Number of the Beast

Produced by Martin 'Farmer' Birch
Released 22 March 1982
Highest chart position and certification at 1/double platinum (UK), 33/platinum (US)
Featuring Steve Harris (bass), Dave Murray (guitar), Clive Burr (drums), Adrian Smith (guitar), Bruce Dickinson (vocals)

Contrary to popular belief these days, *The Number of the Beast* was not universally acclaimed upon its release in 1982. Critical opinion was divided, with the *Rolling Stone* review calling the album close to 'dreadfully bland', and the backlash from the religious right in the United States of America was quite severe. However, in retrospect it is obvious that *The Number of the Beast* was Iron Maiden's giant leap into the biggest league of hard rock music, becoming their first number 1 charter in the UK and their first million-seller in the USA.

The build-up had been shaky. In September 1981, Iron Maiden and their manager Rod Smallwood decided to part ways with singer Paul Di'Anno, and in his place they recruited the very different and very creative Bruce Dickinson. Changing the singer and frontman is a risky endeavour for any band, but Di'Anno had become a liability for a Maiden that was charging into what would become the classic era of their career. Iron Maiden needed a singer less prone to the sex and drugs part of their environment, and band leader Steve Harris took the opportunity to upgrade with a voice that matched his vision for the future music of his band. After debuting their new singer with a few concerts in Italy and England in late 1981, Maiden set about recording their new album in a mad rush from January into February of 1982.

It might be hard to believe today, but the ground-breaking *The Number of the Beast* album was recorded and mixed in just five weeks. In the safe hands of producer Martin Birch, Iron Maiden once again recorded at London's Battery Studios, which gives *The Number of the Beast* a sound quite similar to its predecessor *Killers*. Maiden had touring commitments coming up, and Birch worked days and nights to get everything ready for a single release to precede the album, all pretty much in time for the start of the tour. Nigel Green (then known as Nigel Hewitt-Green) would assist Birch at the console, as he had done for *Killers*.

A noticeable development from the first two Iron Maiden albums is the diversity that now begins to creep into the band's songwriting, with Adrian Smith slotting into place as a tonal alternative to Steve Harris, and an uncredited Bruce Dickinson also making his presence felt in both the music and the lyrics of Maiden's new album. Dickinson was reportedly barred from contributing due to a publishing contract that his former band Samson still had him tied to, but the singer would make what he cheekily calls 'moral contributions' to several of the new songs that Harris and Smith were working up in late 1981. It was the start of a fruitful collaboration between the three of them that would produce a great amount of classic hard rock and heavy metal music throughout the 1980s. *The Number of The Beast* is the sound of a band with everything to prove and the proper skills available to do it.

The musical confidence of the new Dickinson-era Iron Maiden would be mirrored in the outstanding cover artwork by Derek Riggs. A painting that had originally been intended for the previous year's 'Purgatory' single, the image sees Eddie puppeteering the Devil who is puppeteering Eddie, in a hellish landscape of fire and brimstone. Eddie is still recognizable as the character on the *Killers* cover, but his environment has changed from the realistic (city streets in England) to the fantastic (well, Hell). Maiden and Smallwood might not have meant to court controversy, but the album title and artwork sure made it a likely attraction.

'INVADERS'

Not to be confused with the earlier Steve Harris composition 'Invasion' that appeared on both *The Soundhouse Tapes* in 1979 and on the B-side to the 'Women in Uniform' single in 1980, this is Harris' 1982 take at adapting the Viking sackings of Britain into a heavy metal song. Never performed live by the band, 'Invaders' is most memorable for the way new singer Bruce Dickinson delivers the nearly unsingable lyrics with such panache. As entertaining as it is, and as fired up as the band sounds, the Harris song itself would pale in comparison with most other tracks on *The Number of the Beast*.

'Children of the Damned'

This is the song that clearly makes a statement about the future of Iron Maiden with their new singer. Written by Steve Harris, with some input from Bruce Dickinson (probably the lyrics, one would assume), 'Children of the Damned' is a haunting song that begins with quiet acoustic chords and a beautiful guitar melody. Inspired by the film *Village of the Damned* from 1960 (based on the John Wyndham novel *The Midwich Cuckoos*) and its 1964 sequel *Children of the Damned*, this is Maiden stretching out into the realms of horror and science fiction storytelling that would come to characterise their 1980s era.

After the second chorus the song breaks into a faster pace. Here comes a thrilling minor third harmony guitar section and then Adrian Smith's spellbinding lead guitar spot of melodic tapping. When the song resolves into the wordless Dickinson chant that seems tailor-made for audience participation, and the final lyrical drama of 'You're children of the damned / Like candles, watch them burn', the listener is left both exhausted and deeply satisfied by one of the most fully realised Iron Maiden mini-epics to date. After the 1982 *Beast on the Road* tour the song would be rare in concert setlists, but it did make notable returns on the *Somewhere in Time* tour in 1986 and *The Book of Souls* tour in 2016.

'The Prisoner'

The previous song was clearly not a lucky one-off. After a spoken word intro lifted from the television series that inspired the song, 'The Prisoner' kicks off with a drumbeat devised by Bruce Dickinson and a guitar riff by Adrian Smith. Steve Harris would also chip in, and the result would be a triumphantly melodic and dramatic heavy metal track that is most of all defined by its glorious chorus of 'Not a prisoner / I'm a free man'. To build a sense of drama after the second chorus, the song breaks down into a section of rhythm accents over which Adrian Smith plays a beautiful arpeggio pattern that eventually leads into his solo and a hand-off to Murray's solo. 'The Prisoner' would become a rarity in Maiden's setlist, but it was successfully featured on the 1988 *Seventh Son of a Seventh Son* tour and returned for the *Maiden England World Tour* in 2012 and *The Future Past Tour* in 2023.

'22 Acacia Avenue'

The story of the prostitute Charlotte that began with 'Charlotte the Harlot' on *Iron Maiden* in 1980 continues here with the disclosure that she renders her services from the address 22 Acacia Avenue. The equal parts embarrassing and disturbing lyrics by Harris are attached to music mainly written by Smith. In fact, some of the riffs and melodies in '22 Acacia Avenue' are sourced from a song that Harris had seen Smith perform with his previous band Urchin years earlier. When Maiden were working up material for *The Number of the Beast*, Harris hummed some of it to Smith and asked if they could rework that tune for Maiden. The second part of the Charlotte saga was a concert regular in 1982 to 1984 but would be a rare feature after that.

'THE NUMBER OF THE BEAST'

Steve Harris had a bad dream, and he turned it into a great song. Partially inspired by the 1978 supernatural horror film *Damien: Omen II*, the spoken word opening from the Bible's 'Book of Revelation' gives way to a major key bass and guitar riff that supports Dickinson's dramatic delivery of the first verse: 'I left alone / My mind was blank / I needed time to think, to get the memories from my mind', and so on with great passion.

The song is a furious rocker that has been included in every Iron Maiden concert setlist since its release, except the 2006 *A Matter of Life and Death* tour and the 2023–24 *Future Past* tour, and it would be picked as the second single from the album in April 1982. It could be called deceptively simple, as the opening and ending riff is not in the straight ahead 4/4 time signature but a trickier 4/4 plus 6/4, and even so the song serves to get audiences worked up and singing along to the mischievous '666' chorus. The major key is a particular point of interest here: Already shown off in the choruses to 'Invaders' and 'The Prisoner', major keys are quite prolific on *The Number of the Beast* (another example being the next song coming up) but not really that common throughout the Iron Maiden catalogue.

'RUN TO THE HILLS'

Producer Martin Birch picked 'Run to the Hills' as the first single, which preceded the album in February 1982 and became a UK hit at number 7 in the singles chart. Another track in a major key, 'Run to the Hills' is a Harris song that features Dickinson's uncredited musical and lyrical input. The subject is the European migration westwards across the North American continent and the tragic effects of this exploration and colonisation on Native Americans. The song has been a common feature in Maiden's concert setlists throughout their career, originally appearing early in the 1982 set but quickly settling as a regular encore. Derek Riggs' artwork for the 'Run to the Hills' single cover depicts Eddie and Satan doing battle in front of the hordes of hell, while the artwork for subsequent single 'The Number of the Beast' shows that Eddie won, holding out the severed head of the Devil. This was the first instance where Riggs painted a multi-part story where the album cover and single covers tie in with each other in a sequence.

'GANGLAND'

You can bet that for every Maiden song in existence there will be more than a few fans hailing it as their best. This is probably also the case with 'Gangland', a by-the-numbers early 1980s metal tune that feels much less innovative than most of the songs on *The Number of the Beast*. Along with opener 'Invaders' it has never been performed in concert, and both Harris and Dickinson regret putting it on the album instead of 'Total Eclipse', the 'Run to the Hills' single B-side. While the music of 'Gangland' was co-written by Smith and drummer Clive Burr, with Burr's likely contribution being the energetic drum patterns, odds are that the lyrics were written by an uncredited Dickinson.

'HALLOWED BE THY NAME'

Often appearing at the very top of lists of the best Iron Maiden songs, 'Hallowed Be Thy Name' built on the epic style of the first album's 'Phantom of the Opera' and would serve as Steve Harris' own measure of direction when he crafted yet longer and more intricate epics to come. The lyrics present the thoughts of a condemned man who is awaiting his hanging, and Dickinson perfectly conveys the sorrow and anxiety across Harris' rollercoaster arrangement from a quiet intro to the all-out metal bombast of the closing chorus.

'Hallowed Be Thy Name' has in later years been the subject of a plagiarism lawsuit where people behind the band Beckett accused Maiden of ripping off parts of their song 'Life's Shadow' from 1974 for both 'Hallowed Be Thy Name' and the later track 'The Nomad' on the *Brave New World* album in 2000. The suit was settled out of court for a reported 100 000 GBP. 'Hallowed Be Thy Name' was absent from the Iron Maiden setlist for the very first time since its release in 2012 to 2014 for unknown reasons, and subsequently in 2017 because of the plagiarism lawsuit, but it has since returned as a regular and remains one of Maiden's most popular songs despite being left out again on the 2023–24 *Future Past* tour.

RELATED RECORDINGS

'Total Eclipse' is an original track featured on the B-side of the 'Run to the Hills' single. It was written by Dave Murray and Steve Harris in some kind of collaboration with drummer Clive Burr, and it is yet another instance of suspiciously Dickinson-esque lyrics showing up without him being publicly credited. Whatever the case, both Harris and Dickinson are on record saying that they regret not putting this song on the album in place of 'Gangland'. But 'Total Eclipse' is not really a much better track, being somewhat reminiscent of run-of-the-mill Judas Priest riffs of the era and not in the same ground-breaking league as most of the songs on *The Number of the Beast*. 'Total Eclipse' would be added to the Japanese edition of the album in 1982, following 'Run to the Hills' in the track listing. It would later appear on the 1998 CD remaster as next-to-last ahead of 'Hallowed Be Thy Name', and finally on the 2022 vinyl release *The Number of the Beast over Hammersmith* in place of 'Gangland'.

The B-side to second single 'The Number of the Beast' was a concert version of the *Iron Maiden* track 'Remember Tomorrow (live)' recorded in Padua, Italy at one of the first Maiden concerts to feature Bruce Dickinson, at the tail-end of the 1981 *Killers* tour in October 1981.

The early 1980s was an age long before the live album became as commonplace as in later Maiden days when they would release one every three or four years. Even so, in early 1982 Maiden and Smallwood conceived of the idea to film and record their London show at Hammersmith Odeon on 20 March for a concert video. Ultimately, the results were scrapped because the stage was not properly lit for capture on film cameras, although some songs showed up on the 1987 retrospective video *12 Wasted Years*. However, the soundtrack, mixed by front-of-house engineer Doug Hall, sounded incredible. Had live albums been more common at the time, this would surely have been Maiden's first. As it happens, it did not see the light of day in its entirety until the 2002 box set *Eddie's Archive*, where a double CD is dedicated to what by then would be called *Beast over Hammersmith*. The band sounds on absolute top form in this performance, and it is a unique experience to hear them blast through new songs from *The Number of the Beast* that had not yet been released. The spoken word intro to the title track, for example, is met with dead silence from an audience completely unfamiliar with what is coming up. By the time the 1982 tour was over, producer Martin Birch's prediction had come true, and Iron Maiden's *The Number of the Beast* had become a huge album. In 2022, Maiden released a heavyweight triple vinyl edition of the remastered album from 2015 plus the Hammersmith concert in a package title *The Number of the Beast over Hammersmith*. Knowing that there are other great concert recordings in the band's vaults, including the Reading 1982 performance that is also featured in *Eddie's Archive*, it is to be hoped that a deluxe box set of this classic Maiden album will someday be available.

Listening preferences

As a rule, Iron Maiden albums sound great in their original 1980s editions. For *The Number of the Beast* this means either the vinyl releases from 1982 and throughout the decade, or the early CD releases, first of which was the

Japanese edition in 1986. The hiccup occurs with the 1998 CD remaster, where the lack of dynamic range makes the album sound harsher and less well-rounded than Birch's mix. This problem was rectified to a satisfying degree with the 2014 heavyweight vinyl reissue, which was pressed from the original 1982 master, and the 2015 digital remaster, which is the version currently available on CD and streaming services.

4

Piece of Mind

Produced by Martin 'Black Night' Birch
Released 16 May 1983
Highest chart position and certification at 3/platinum (UK), 14/platinum (US)
Featuring Steve Harris (bass), Dave Murray (guitar), Adrian Smith (guitar), Bruce Dickinson (vocals), Nicko McBrain (drums)

The Number of the Beast had given Iron Maiden their international breakthrough and made the members of the band millionaires. To protect their finances from the excessive high-earner income tax in the UK at the time, Maiden's management (Rod Smallwood and by now his partner Andy Taylor) advised the band to record their next albums abroad. Combined with their international touring, this would keep them out of their home country most of the year and not eligible for taxes.

As a result of this, Iron Maiden began their mid-1980s routine of writing music in the Channel Islands at the start of the year before recording their new songs at Compass Point Studios in Nassau, Bahamas. The new working environment was one of two factors that brought a significant change of sound from the previous couple of Maiden albums. The other factor was a new drummer: Nicko McBrain. His predecessor Clive Burr was fired from the band at the end of the 1982 tour, and McBrain was the final piece of the puzzle that completed Steve Harris' classic era Iron Maiden line-up.

The *Piece of Mind* album, once again produced by the great Martin Birch and recorded with the working title *Food for Thought*, is one of the most impressive entries in the Maiden catalogue. Seemingly suffering no pressure to follow up *The Number of the Beast*, the band sounds utterly inspired and overflowing with creativity. The addition of McBrain to the line-up sets Harris' imagination free to conceive whatever musical flights of fancy with complete confidence in his band's abilities, and by now there is also the impact of the synergy between guitarist Adrian Smith and singer Bruce Dickinson, who would co-write some of the greatest Maiden material from this point on. *Piece of Mind* is the earliest Iron Maiden record that Steve Harris regularly cites as one of his personal favourites. As he said in the official Mick Wall biography of the band, 'You can nearly always go back to an album and pick out things you might have done differently, but I still think *Piece of Mind* is good the way it is.'

The ensuing *World Piece Tour* in 1983 was Iron Maiden's first as international headliners. The previous tour had seen them headlining in most countries while settling for support positions in North America, but manager Smallwood decided to push his band as headliners everywhere in 1983, including the US, and reaped massive rewards. Maiden came out of this trial by fire having secured their status as arena headliners (even selling out New York City's Madison Square Garden along the way), and the single 'Flight of Icarus' would be their most popular radio track of all time in the US. While not charting as high as *The Number of the Beast* in the UK or most European countries, *Piece of Mind* would increase the band's global record sales and keep Maiden on the upward trajectory. It is worth noting that chart positions don't necessarily give a clear indication of sales over time, and Iron Maiden was always a band that played the long game rather than chasing hits.

The musical sophistication of classic era Iron Maiden is also reflected in the artwork for *Piece of Mind* and its accompanying singles. Regular illustrator Derek Riggs is moving Eddie out of his earlier environments of city streets and hellish landscapes. In the 'Flight of Icarus' single artwork, Eddie has built himself wings to escape from Hell, and he torches the hubristic Icarus on his way out. However, the mysterious box in the sky is about to incarcerate Eddie for a horrifying lobotomy, the aftermath of which is presented on the *Piece of Mind* album cover itself, a snarling Eddie restrained in a straitjacket and chained to the walls and floor, just a few feet away from escape through the open door into the ether. The dynamic of Maiden's lyrical and conceptual ideas and Riggs' twisted imagination offers up its most perfect combo of music and imagery to date with the *Piece of Mind* cycle.

'WHERE EAGLES DARE'

A big drum spectacle heralds the coming of Nicko McBrain, and the dawn of a new era in Iron Maiden's career and sound. 'Where Eagles Dare', written by Steve Harris, is the band's most ambitious opening number yet, a flurry of riffs and harmonies over a Maiden-ised shuffle beat, with Bruce Dickinson's operatic tenor delivering the supreme drama of a fictional World War II rescue mission in the German Alps. The song's middle section is noteworthy, where conventional guitar solos are overtaken by reverb-heavy licks and dive-bombs and harmony runs courtesy of the adventurous Dave Murray and Adrian Smith, all of it backed by producer Martin Birch's subtle use of machine gun fire sound effects.

Inspired by the Clint Eastwood-starring film *Where Eagles Dare* from 1968, for which Scottish author Alistair MacLean wrote the screenplay while concurrently writing his novel of the same name, 'Where Eagles Dare' was the impressive opening song on the *Piece of Mind* tour. Making significant demands of McBrain's skill set, particularly the speed and agility of his right foot on the bass drum pedal, few bands of that time could muster anything as dramatic and at the same time melodically satisfying. The song would return to the set in 1986 (with Dickinson in less than top form) and 1993 (with Smith absent from the band), before making its hugely anticipated modern-day comebacks on the *Early Days* tour in 2005 and the *Legacy of the Beast* tour in 2018.

'Revelations'

By now it becomes abundantly clear that any vestiges of Iron Maiden's more primitive roots that were evident on all their previous three records are completely removed. 'Revelations' is a song steeped in progressive rock tradition: unexpected time-changes abound, while conventional rock song structure is ignored with glee and enthusiasm. It is simply impossible to imagine this track with either Dennis Stratton, Paul Di'Anno, or even Clive Burr. The performance quality of the latest Iron Maiden line-up surpasses all.

'Revelations' was Bruce Dickinson's first official songwriting credit on an Iron Maiden album, although he contributed unofficially on *The Number of the Beast* the year before. This song is credited to the singer alone and is essentially his first masterpiece. Influenced by the life and work of Aleister Crowley while also quoting a passage from the G. K. Chesterton hymn 'O God of Earth and Altar', 'Revelations' is the first example of Dickinson's career-long fascination with the occult, which would serve him well both in and out of Maiden. The song would be retired from Maiden's concert setlists after 1985 but it would make a welcome return in 2003 to become a semi-regular feature in later years.

'Flight of Icarus'

A prime example of what Maiden gained with the Smith/Dickinson writing partnership, 'Flight of Icarus' was the first single from *Piece of Mind*, released in April 1983. It is also the highest-charting Maiden song of all time in the US, peaking at number 8 in the Billboard Top Album Tracks chart that ranked songs by measuring radio airplay. Dickinson would sometimes suggest that Harris never liked 'Flight of Icarus', but Harris would refute this and claim that he simply preferred the live version over the studio recording.

The song's creation started with Smith's chord sequence for the chorus, to which Dickinson added a melody that would be multi-tracked in all its harmony glory. The Dickinson lyrics take a revisionist view of the ambition and tragedy in the tale of the young man Icarus of Greek mythology, who flies too close to the sun on wings of wax and feathers, plunging to his death when the wings catch on fire. 'Flight of Icarus' was a concert staple in the years 1983 to 1986, but it would then disappear for an inexplicably long time, before finally being resurrected on the *Legacy of the Beast* tour in 2018, all of thirty-two years later.

'DIE WITH YOUR BOOTS ON'

This is the first official writing collaboration between Smith, Dickinson, and Harris. A melodic riff-fest, 'Die with Your Boots On' sounds as relentless as its title implies. The high-register vocal performance from Dickinson is particularly astounding, while Smith and his guitar partner Murray deliver all the lead and harmony work that fans desire, even the opening main riff of the song being played as a minor third harmony. 'Die with Your Boots On' would appear in concert setlists throughout the band's history, but only at rare intervals.

'THE TROOPER'

What was called side two in the days of vinyl kicks off with one of the most popular Iron Maiden songs of all time, and certainly in the age of streaming. 'The Trooper' was composed by Harris and released as the second single from *Piece of Mind* in June 1983. Inspired by Alfred Tennyson's 1854 poem 'The Charge of the Light Brigade', which discusses the Battle of the Balaclava during the Crimean War in the 1850s, the song utilises the patented Maiden gallop to great effect. There is plenty of the minor third harmony guitars and a great singalong harmony chant in place of a conventional chorus. 'The Trooper' is the *Piece of Mind* track that has been present in most of the band's setlists through the decades.

'STILL LIFE'

Dave Murray's writing credits were few and far between in the 1980s. There was 'Charlotte the Harlot' on *Iron Maiden* in 1980, but then his subsequent efforts ('Twilight Zone' in 1981 and 'Total Eclipse' in 1982) were relegated to single B-sides. 'Still Life' might be the connoisseur's choice of all Murray songs, its dark, yet compelling mood maintained throughout, from the quiet intro via the chilling choruses ('Nightmares, forever calling me') to its intricate middle section where Murray trades solo spots with Smith.

A fun footnote is the backwards message before the start of the song, which is in fact an inebriated McBrain impersonating the Ugandan despot Idi Amin, all done to wind up people who were freaking out about Maiden's supposedly Satanic intentions in the wake of *The Number of the Beast*. Otherwise, Harris' lyrics are seemingly inspired by J. Ramsey Campbell's short horror story 'The Inhabitant of the Lake' from 1964. 'Still Life' would only feature in the early UK and European legs of the 1983 *World Piece Tour*, being dropped once the US leg started. It made a brief comeback for the final UK leg of the *Seventh Son of a Seventh Son* tour in late 1988, thereby being immortalised in the *Maiden England* video, but it has not been heard since.

'Quest for Fire'
Probably the most obscure and divisive song on *Piece of Mind*, this is a Harris composition that people seem to either love or hate. The lyrics are loosely based on the 1981 film *Quest for Fire*, itself an adaptation of a 1911 novel, and 'loosely' is probably a kind assessment since Harris describes the film's late Stone Age setting as 'a time when dinosaurs walked the Earth', which it certainly wasn't. The music marches along in a slow shuffle, as it builds to a highlight: the harmony guitar section that opens up into a blistering Smith solo and then one of the most effortlessly uplifting Murray solos on any Iron Maiden record. 'Quest for Fire' was one of only two *Piece of Mind* tracks not performed on tour, but even at its arguable low point, this album maintains a very high standard.

'Sun and Steel'
Another catchy and melodic proposition from Smith and Dickinson, 'Sun and Steel' is probably the *Piece of Mind* song you will be surprised to learn that the band has never performed in concert. The track lifts its title from a 1968 essay by Japanese poet Yukio Mishima, who wrote about his experiences with martial arts, and is further inspired by the life of the samurai Miyamoto Musashi in the early 1600s. Thematically, it would have been very much at home on 2021's *Senjutsu*, and it is an early indication of Dickinson's personal interest in sword fighting.

'To Tame a Land'
Written by Harris, 'To Tame a Land' is the first explicit example of Maiden music built on the Middle Eastern Persian scale or the corresponding Indian raga, something that would also be a pronounced feature of the subsequent *Powerslave* record. Signing off from *Piece of Mind* with this massive and sinister epic, Harris points ahead to the next album and lets the band flex its progressive muscles. Heavy riffs and tasteful melodies conjure desert landscapes, and Dickinson proves that there is no tongue-twisting lyric too

weird for him to translate into classic metal. Indeed, the singer's performance of this track on the *World Piece Tour* was regularly spellbinding, elevating Maiden and their repertoire above and beyond their contemporaries in hard rock and heavy metal music. Its only realistic chance to reappear in a setlist was probably the 2005 *Early Days* tour, but it was sadly not included.

The convoluted lyrics of 'To Tame a Land', which demand all of Dickinson's skill to come across to an audience, are based on Frank Herbert's classic science fiction novel *Dune* from 1965. The band shied away from calling the track 'Dune' when they learned from Herbert's representatives that he would not take kindly to being quoted by them. For the subsequent record's closing epic, Harris would sensibly turn to literary materials that were old enough not to be hampered by copyrights.

Related recordings
Maiden recorded the Montrose song 'I've Got the Fire' for the B-side of the 'Flight of Icarus' single, a song they had performed regularly in their early days and previously issued as a live B-side to the 'Sanctuary' single in 1980. This 1983 studio version features a particularly fired up performance by Dickinson, making the Paul Di'Anno era recede far into the background. For the B-side to second single 'The Trooper', Maiden recorded 'Cross-Eyed Mary', a Jethro Tull song from their 1971 *Aqualung* album. One of Tull's most riffy tracks, it suits Maiden well, although having the vocal register an octave above Ian Anderson's baritone turned out to be a little extreme even for Dickinson...

Listening preferences
Piece of Mind is one of the Iron Maiden records that sounds overwhelmingly brilliant in its original vinyl edition, making the numerous 1983 or 1984 pressings worth checking out. The US version was mastered by legendary mastering engineer George Marino at Sterling Sound, New York City. The original CD editions from the late 1980s and early 1990s also sound good, even if sometimes a little light on the bass frequencies, while the 1998 remaster is predictably too loud across all frequencies. The 2014 heavyweight vinyl and the 2015 digital remaster both sound good, although they are no match for the original vinyl edition.

5
Powerslave

Produced by Martin 'Pool Bully' Birch
Released 3 September 1984
Highest chart position and certification at 2/gold (UK), 12/platinum (US)
Featuring Steve Harris (bass), Dave Murray (guitar), Adrian Smith (guitar), Bruce Dickinson (vocals), Nicko McBrain (drums)

The *Powerslave* album marked the pinnacle of Iron Maiden's classic era, particularly in the USA. Maiden and their manager Rod Smallwood had laid the groundwork with extensive North American touring in 1981 and 1982, as support act for the likes of Judas Priest, Rainbow, and the Scorpions, before moving into headlining their own tour in 1983. This primed their audience for the release of *Powerslave* in 1984 and the massive *World Slavery Tour* that would stay mostly on US soil and culminate in the classic *Live After Death* double live album and concert video in 1985. Maiden's global sales kept increasing at this time, even if the UK and US certifications cited at the top of each chapter do not necessarily reflect this. Certifications, after all, had to be purchased by either the artist or the record company (EMI in Maiden's case) and this was not always done even when sales merited the award.

As with their previous record *Piece of Mind*, Iron Maiden began 1984 with writing sessions on the cold and stormy island of Jersey in the Channel Islands between France and England, before moving on to the much warmer and more comfortable Bahamas to record their new music in Compass Point Studios, Nassau. Regular producer Martin Birch would mix the recordings in New York City's fabled Electric Lady Studios, as he had previously done with *Piece of Mind* the year before. Birch would later state that he found the

Compass Point facilities to be 'pretty bare bones' compared with studios in New York or Los Angeles, but that mixing at Electric Lady alleviated most of the problems this caused.

Marking the first time Iron Maiden recorded a second album with an unchanged line-up, *Powerslave* practically bursts with the sound of a band full of self-confidence. It could be argued that the material was more cohesively impressive on *Piece of Mind*, but *Powerslave* is certainly the height of Maiden's guitar-driven heavy metal sound. Indeed, guitarists Dave Murray and Adrian Smith are on excellent form throughout, as is the rhythm combo of bassist Steve Harris and drummer Nicko McBrain, and singer Bruce Dickinson delivers his by now customary operatics to distinguish Maiden's metal from anything else on offer in the mid-1980s. The band and Smallwood took advantage of Maiden's prestige by booking and extending their 1984–85 tour into the month of July in the summer of 1985, making everyone (and Dickinson in particular) burned out to the point of risking the future of the band if a time-out was not called.

If Iron Maiden had become slaves to the power of their own success, as Dickinson would suggest is the cheeky point of the symbolism in his 'Powerslave' lyrics, the concept of that song would also seed the incredible Derek Riggs album artwork that depicts Eddie now having become a mythical pharaoh in ancient Egypt. This artwork would in turn be the basis for the stage production of the *World Slavery Tour*, a concept and execution which is still thought of as possibly the greatest that Maiden ever staged. By this point in the mid-1980s, Iron Maiden had become the world's biggest metal band (notwithstanding the softer rock of Van Halen or Def Leppard or the emerging Bon Jovi) and they would be the yardstick by which everyone else, including Metallica, would measure their own ideas.

'Aces High'

Iron Maiden's most celebrated opener of all time is Steve Harris' thrilling composition about the Battle of Britain in 1940, when Nazi Germany's air force, the Luftwaffe, brought terror bombing to English cities and battled it out in the skies with Britain's Royal Air Force. In concert, the song would be preceded by an excerpt from Prime Minister Winston Churchill's legendary speech, 'We shall go on to the end…' and so forth, given right after the dramatic evacuation of Dunkirk in France. This period from the summer of 1940 and into early 1941 was in certain ways the darkest hour of the Second World War, when it looked all but assured that Hitler's forces would trample all of Europe in fascist victory.

'Aces High' is a fast and furious call to arms, replete with acrobatic Dickinson vocals and patented Murray and Smith lead and harmony guitars. It was released in October 1984 as the second single from *Powerslave*, with

Derek Riggs' Eddie in the cockpit of a Spitfire plane in mid-battle. After being the opening track on the 1984–85 *World Slavery Tour* and the *Live After Death* concert album, the song returned as opener in the Maiden set on the 1999 reunion tour, the 2008–09 *Somewhere Back in Time* tour, and the 2018–19 *Legacy of the Beast* tour, while also (more surprisingly) taking the spot of first encore on the *Maiden England* tour in 2012 to 2014, and then as final encore on the 2022 part of the *Legacy of the Beast* tour. Most recently it once again opened the encore section on the fiftieth anniversary *Run for Your Lives* tour in 2025.

'2 Minutes to Midnight'

Following the lead single 'Flight of Icarus' from the *Piece of Mind* album, the release of '2 Minutes to Midnight' as the lead from *Powerslave* in August 1984 established the tradition of profiling upcoming Iron Maiden albums with an Adrian Smith composition. As before, the lyrics and melodies are Bruce Dickinson's, and as Smith would later state in the band's official biography, 'I had the right riff and Bruce had the right words.' It becomes evident that the collaboration of these two songwriters was giving Maiden a commercial edge that complemented Harris' often more idiosyncratic works in fine style. This juxtaposition of aesthetics should not be underestimated in the appraisal of Iron Maiden's success.

But Smith can hardly be credited for inventing the song's opening riff. An earlier track with a nearly identical riff is White Spirit's 'Midnight Chaser' from 1980, co-written by their guitarist Janick Gers, who would of course later join Iron Maiden. Another song in 1980 with a nearly identical riff is Budgie's 'Wild Fire', and there is also the 1981 Riot song 'Swords and Tequila' and Accept's 'Flash Rockin' Man' from 1982, to name just a few. Iron Maiden's '2 Minutes to Midnight' would become the most famous iteration of this riff thanks to the high quality of the rest of the song, including Dickinson's lyrics about war as greedy business and the title's reference to the Doomsday Clock that describes the likelihood of global catastrophe caused by humans. '2 Minutes to Midnight' is the *Powerslave* song that has appeared most regularly in Maiden's concert setlists over the years.

'Losfer Words (Big 'Orra)'

After a strong opening the *Powerslave* album takes a puzzling dive with this Harris instrumental. Complete with the joke title that says, 'Lost for words (big horror)', the competence of the performances cannot conceal the fact that the track is merely filler to pad out the running time of an album that would be better off without it. The song would be performed regularly on the 1984 European leg of the *World Slavery Tour*, but it is hard to imagine a pointless track like this on either *The Number of the Beast* or *Piece of Mind*.

'FLASH OF THE BLADE'

Besides teaming up with Smith for great single material like '2 Minutes to Midnight', Dickinson would also write songs on his own. Never performed live, 'Flash of the Blade' is lyrically in the tradition of the previous album's 'Sun and Steel', a paean to life by the sword. Dickinson also provides plenty of neoclassical harmony parts for Murray and Smith to arrange in the song's middle section. However, at this point the *Powerslave* album begins to feel a little overbearing, and the absence of counterbalancing songs like 'Children of the Damned' or 'Revelations' (on *The Number of the Beast* and *Piece of Mind*, respectively) renders the first half of the album somewhat one-dimensional.

'THE DUELLISTS'

The best of the obscure songs on *Powerslave*, and one that has sadly never been performed by the band in concert, is Harris' 'The Duellists'. Another track in the bassist's highly valued quick shuffle beat, like 'Phantom of the Opera' and 'Where Eagles Dare' before it, this song has plenty of dramatic vocal delivery and even a melodically tender middle section where Murray and Smith settle a three-part guitar harmony between them. The comparison to 'Where Eagles Dare' is pertinent in that the verses of the latter has Dickinson singing a descending line that is mirrored in the verses of 'The Duellists' as an ascending line, almost note for note. However good 'The Duellists' might be, it is unfortunately hampered by being yet another song of swordsmanship following hard on the heels of 'Flash of the Blade'. Dickinson's latter sings of 'One man and his honour', while the Harris counterpart goes 'Oh, fight for the honour'. The track-by-track inventiveness and surplus of ideas that the band showed on *Piece of Mind* regresses noticeably on several of the *Powerslave* songs.

'BACK IN THE VILLAGE'

Maiden played this song at their first couple of *Powerslave* shows in Poland in August 1984, but it was then dropped and never returned. 'Back in the Village' opens what used to be side two in the days of vinyl much like 'Aces High' had opened side one, fast and furious, but it is not in the same league in terms of narrative drama and melodic appeal. Written by the Smith and Dickinson duo, 'Back in the Village' is frantic and guitar-driven, continuing the *Powerslave* album's relentless heavy metal pursuit and giving no respite from the fury. The best sonic quality of *Powerslave* is the way that Murray and Smith by now have perfected the well-balanced guitar tone so essential to classic Maiden music, where Murray's Stratocasters are deftly complemented by Smith's arsenal of Les Pauls, Lados and Ibanezes.

'POWERSLAVE'

The chief reason why *Powerslave* is generally regarded as one of the greatest Iron Maiden albums is to be found towards the end of the record. The last two tracks stand out as all-time progressive heavy metal masterpieces, the first of which is Dickinson's title track 'Powerslave' itself. Dickinson presented the band with two separate compositions: the main sections of the song's verses and choruses, and the quiet middle section that erupts into the triumphant guitar solo and three-part harmony cascade. Harris suggested that Dickinson simply glue the two ideas together for one epic track.

The lyrics tell a chilling and possibly allegorical tale of a pharaoh's addiction to power in ancient Egypt, and the song would inspire the fantastic Derek Riggs cover art for the album and the massive stage production of the *World Slavery Tour*. 'Powerslave' was a cornerstone in this set, complete with a walk-on Mummy Eddie to excite the audience, but it would then disappear until its resurrection on the 1999 reunion tour. The song made a highly anticipated comeback on the *Somewhere Back in Time* tour in 2008, and a more surprising appearance on the 2016 *The Book of Souls* tour. Most recently it featured on the fiftieth anniversary *Run for Your Lives* tour in 2025, aided by an impressive video and pyro production.

'RIME OF THE ANCIENT MARINER'

The album's crowning achievement is 'Rime of the Ancient Mariner', the Steve Harris composition that clocks in at a massive 14 minutes. The song is based on, and quotes extensively from, Samuel Taylor Coleridge's epic 1798 poem about a cursed seafarer's encounter with a ghost ship. Harris began writing this track when Maiden rehearsed in the Channel Islands in early 1984, but he would not manage to pull it all together until they hit crunch time in their Bahamas studio, lyric sheets reportedly covering a wall from floor to ceiling and an enchanted Harris convincing his band of the composition's merits.

The first part of the song chugs along in a familiar Iron Maiden gallop over which Dickinson tells the tale in classic fashion, 'Hear the rime of the ancient mariner / See his eye as he stops one of three / Mesmerizes one of the wedding guests / Stay here and listen to the nightmares of the sea'. The drama intensifies with a time change that quickens the pace before the bone-chilling quiet middle section where Murray and Smith conjure up foggy seas and creaking ships with their atmospheric guitar work. The track climaxes with a shuffle beat solo and harmony guitars section, and then settles down to a resolution in the same gallop as the opening, 'And the wedding guest's a sad and wiser man / And the tale goes on and on and on and on'. Maiden's lyrics are by now firmly rooted in fantasy, poetry, and history, making the Paul Di'Anno era but a distant memory.

'Rime of the Ancient Mariner' redefined the Maiden epic, building on 'Phantom of the Opera', 'Hallowed Be Thy Name' and 'To Tame a Land' before it. After this point every long and self-consciously epic and narrative-driven track the band ever attempted would inevitably be compared to 'Mariner'. The song was the other cornerstone of the *World Slavery Tour* live show, alongside 'Powerslave', and it would remain in the setlist on the subsequent tour for *Somewhere in Time* in 1986–87. It reappeared triumphantly for the 2008–09 *Somewhere Back in Time* tour, and then again for the fiftieth anniversary *Run for Your Lives* tour in 2025.

Related recordings

On the B-side of the '2 Minutes to Midnight' single is 'Rainbow's Gold', a cover of the 1974 track 'A Rainbow's Gold' by the band Beckett. Songwriters behind Beckett were plaintiffs in the 2017 plagiarism lawsuit against Maiden for 'Hallowed Be Thy Name', and the original Beckett version of 'Rainbow's Gold' was sung by vocalist Terry Slesser, who had auditioned to replace Paul Di'Anno in 1981. Maiden manager Rod Smallwood had also worked as an agent for Beckett in the 1970s, making the Maiden connections obscure but numerous.

On the B-side of the 'Aces High' single is 'King of Twilight', a medley of the two songs 'Crying in the Dark' and 'King of Twilight' by the band Nektar on their 1972 album *A Tab in the Ocean*. Considering the subpar quality of some songs on *Powerslave* it is slightly frustrating to note that it must have taken a few days to rehearse and record 'King of Twilight' and 'Rainbow's Gold' for the single B-sides, time that presumably could have been used to get another killer original song into shape for an album that sorely needed it.

'Mission From 'Arry', a second B-side on the '2 Minutes to Midnight' single, is Bruce Dickinson's secret taping of a row between Steve Harris and a furious Nicko McBrain, after the latter had messed up his drum solo when a roadie futilely tried to tell him to prolong the solo because Harris' bass equipment had broken down and needed time for fixing. Harris defends the hapless roadie, but McBrain is having none of it, and Dickinson finds the whole episode so comical that he turns on a tape recorder.

'The Number of the Beast (live)', a second B-side to the 'Aces High' single, is a concert recording of the song from Dortmund, Germany at the end of the *World Piece Tour* in 1983. The appearance of this track, mixed for release by Martin Birch, suggests that there is a multitrack recording of the entire Dortmund show in the band's archives. The *World Slavery Tour* itself would be documented on *Live After Death*, discussed in the book's part four.

LISTENING PREFERENCES

Like the previous Iron Maiden albums, *Powerslave* sounds great in its earliest vinyl incarnations from the 1980s, but it also sounds quite similar in its 2014 heavyweight vinyl edition, at least to this author's subjective ears. The 1993 Russian reissue on Gala Records should also be mentioned as an outstanding pressing, for the curious collector. The earliest CD editions from the 1980s and early 1990s sound fair if somewhat thin, while the 1998 CD remaster predictably wears your ears out by indulging in the loudness war of overbearing compression and frequency-pushing that was common at that point in time. The 2015 digital remaster, also currently available on CD, is much better but still not as good as the original vinyl edition.

6

Somewhere in Time

Produced by Martin 'Masa' Birch
Released 29 September 1986
Highest chart position and certification at 2/gold (UK), 11/platinum (US)
Featuring Steve Harris (bass), Dave Murray (guitar), Adrian Smith (guitar), Bruce Dickinson (vocals), Nicko McBrain (drums)

After the huge success of *Powerslave* and the *World Slavery Tour* with its resulting *Live After Death* concert album, *Somewhere in Time* was Iron Maiden's overdog challenge: They were top of the heap and expectations of excellence had to be met. This was the third studio album by the classic line-up and Maiden had seen steadily growing success in the United States of America with the records *The Number of the Beast*, *Piece of Mind* and *Powerslave*, as well as *Live After Death*. If there had been pressure for *The Number of the Beast* in 1982 with new vocalist Bruce Dickinson, when many expected them to fail, they now had to deliver in 1986 with a stable line-up, when everyone expected them to succeed.

A well-known schism in the making of *Somewhere in Time* is that between Dickinson and the rest of the band. The singer, still burned out from the *Powerslave* cycle, envisioned a drastic departure in style, making a semi-acoustic Iron Maiden album in a more folk-inspired vein. The proposition was rejected by the rest of the band and their producer Martin Birch, and Maiden went ahead with the two batches of more recognisable hard rock songs that were written by bassist Steve Harris and guitarist Adrian Smith, respectively. This would make *Somewhere in Time* the first Maiden album since *The Number of the Beast* without any Dickinson writing credits, and unlike the latter he did not contribute unofficially this time but resigned himself to being 'just the singer', as he put it, for Maiden's new album.

Somewhere in Time was recorded at Compass Point Studios in Nassau, Bahamas and at Wisseloord Studios in Hilversum, Netherlands. Martin Birch would then mix the recordings at Electric Lady Studios in New York City, as was his routine in the mid-1980s. The album would be Maiden's longest-gestating project to that point, taking about nine months from writing sessions in the Channel Islands in early 1986 to the album's release the following September. Birch's production was this time far removed from the bare-bones aesthetic of the previous couple of studio albums, and the much more lush and layered sound took advantage of new guitar processing that included guitar synthesizers.

The theme of the *Somewhere in Time* album, as the song titles clearly show, is tied together by lyrics that discuss experiences of travelling, space, and time. This concept sees Maiden and regular illustrator Derek Riggs at the height of their visual storytelling, an embellishment of the music that inspired countless young bands in the 1980s. Eddie is now a time-traveling cyborg on a mysterious mission of termination, and this is one of the most iconic and celebrated album artworks in Maiden's history. Such a magnificent creation would probably not be contemplated in our age of thumbnail images, but with the vinyl format it was different. Fans could lose themselves in the obscure details of the front and back sleeve for days, and Riggs would expand the mythology by having Eddie *en route* through space and time in the 'Wasted Years' single artwork, entering a bar post-termination in the 'Stranger in a Strange Land' single artwork, and continuing his journey into unknown future wastelands in the *Somewhere on Tour* artwork.

Building on Iron Maiden's previous progress in the North American market in the years from 1981 to 1985, *Somewhere in Time* ultimately sold over 2 million copies in the United States alone, which qualifies it for a double platinum certification that was never purchased. Commercially speaking, this was the peak of Maiden's US career until the resurgence of their popularity in the post-2000 period.

'Caught Somewhere in Time'

The *Somewhere in Time* album opens with a deep synthesizer chord and a guitar melody with a fifth harmony. The big change of adding synthesizers to the band's sound is immediately apparent and surprisingly successful. 'Caught Somewhere in Time' is a lengthy Steve Harris composition, and among Maiden's album openers it is possibly most comparable to 'Where Eagles Dare' on the *Piece of Mind* album. In other words, it takes its time to build a mood, relying heavily on guitarists Adrian Smith and Dave Murray to weave soundscapes around the rather simple chord patterns. Lyrically the song explores the potential significance of moments in time and choices that lead one way or another. 'Caught Somewhere in Time' was the dramatic opening number on the *Somewhere in Time* tour in 1986–87, and finally returned to the Iron Maiden setlist on the 2023 *The Future Past Tour*, to the immense pleasure of fans who had always felt that the band undervalues this 1986 album.

'Wasted Years'

To a large extent, *Somewhere in Time* is Adrian Smith's album, with both his playing and his writing taking the spotlight like never before. The most prominent example of his ascent, to a certain degree making up for what is lacking in contributions from Bruce Dickinson, is the excellent 'Wasted Years' that was released as the lead single from the album in early September 1986. Writing not only the music, but also the lyrics that deal with homesickness and losing your sense of self and perspective in the routines of touring, Smith delivers what is undoubtedly Iron Maiden's most overtly catchy and commercial song to this point. One of its pleasures is hearing the distinct tone of Smith's voice backing Dickinson's lead vocals in that faultlessly uplifting chorus about living in the moment and letting go of worries.

'Wasted Years', originally titled 'Golden Years', was born during the Channel Islands writing sessions in early 1986, when Harris heard that descending open E string guitar figure purely by accident on Smith's idea tape. When Smith argued, somewhat defensively, that this idea seemed a little too commercial for Maiden, Harris suggested he throw caution to the wind and work it up anyway. 'That night after dinner, I went back to my room and finished the song,' Smith recalls. Preconceived notions discarded, out of this was born one of Maiden's most popular songs, and next to 'Heaven Can Wait' it's the only song from *Somewhere in Time* to appear semi-regularly in their concert setlists over the years, often closing the set on recent tours.

'Sea of Madness'

On the other hand, 'Sea of Madness' proves that it would be a mistake to assume that Adrian Smith writes the commercial-sounding Maiden tunes and not the other types. The opening riff with its open E bass underpinning is a heavy affair, one that was unfortunately never revisited with the later years' six-man line-up of the band. Quite unlike 'Wasted Years', 'Sea of Madness' has blatantly pessimistic lyrics that seem to lament the inevitability of suffering and the unrelenting passage of time, like a river flowing endlessly into the sea. It was permanently retired after the 1986 European leg of the

Somewhere in Time tour, surviving just two gigs into the North American leg in January 1987. The track is groovy, and Dickinson's two-part harmony carries the chorus in style. After the second chorus, the listener is subjected to one of the greatest Iron Maiden guitar solos of all time, Smith capping his own music and lyrics with a goosebump-inducing lead spot that drives home how important he had become to the band.

'Heaven Can Wait'

It could be argued that some of the material on *Somewhere in Time* might have fallen through if it wasn't for the sophistication of Martin Birch's production. The Harris composition 'Heaven Can Wait' would become a live regular, mostly due to its middle section singalong chant and the positive here-and-now message of its lyrics, but it is strictly filler material compared with the rest of the album. It would be the most frequently performed *Somewhere in Time* track in concert, being a staple even through the Blaze Bayley era in the 1990s, but many fans would greatly have preferred other songs from this cherished album to appear in its place, particularly in the decades since Dickinson's return to the band in 1999. It made its most recent appearance, as expected, in the set for *The Future Past Tour* in 2023.

'The Loneliness of the Long Distance Runner'

The second half of *Somewhere in Time* is very moody, and it showcases a sense of variation and dynamics that was missing from much of the previous *Powerslave* album. Side two, as it was in the days of vinyl, opens with Harris' 'The Loneliness of the Long Distance Runner', a track that begins with one of his most affecting guitar melodies of all time. After this quiet intro, with its unorthodox modulation back and forth between E minor and G minor, the song develops into one of the most relentless heavy metal numbers on the album, replete with glorious guitar solos and harmonies that perfectly underline the lyrics' theme of struggling through self-doubt but staying the course to persevere in the long run. 'The Loneliness of the Long Distance Runner', its title possibly lifted from the 1962 movie about self-reliance and escape from physical and emotional constraints, lets us glean a little bit of the Steve Harris philosophy of life. And when the opening guitar melody returns at the end, this time as octaves soaring over the frenetic pace of Nicko McBrain's four snare beats per bar, Maiden bring it home triumphantly. On stage it would be a different matter: The song was performed just once, at the very first concert on the *Somewhere on Tour* in Belgrade in former Yugoslavia, and then dropped for good.

'Stranger in a Strange Land'

The brooding and groovy Smith composition 'Stranger in a Strange Land' was released as the second single from *Somewhere in Time* in November 1986. Founded on a mid-paced gallop reminiscent of 'Wrathchild' and 'Flight of Icarus' before it, 'Stranger in a Strange Land' was written on a gloomy day in the Channel Islands after Smith returned from having a painful root canal treatment at the dentist's office. 'I was looking out at the sea out of the back window of the cab,' Smith would later recall, 'and that riff popped right into my mind.' The vibe of the music fits perfectly with the lyrics, which are not based on the Robert A. Heinlein novel of the same name but inspired by the real-life story of explorer John Torrington. He was a member of the doomed Sir John Franklin expedition into the Arctic in 1845, his eerily well-preserved body exhumed from the ice in 1984. The song tells of an explorer being lost and his remains found, 'preserved in time for all to see', many years later: 'What became of the men that started? / All are gone, and their souls departed'. With this subject matter, Smith convincingly supports the *Somewhere in Time* album title and concept.

The guitar solo is another highlight of the song. Smith has recently explained how this track provided him with his first opportunity to take advantage of some space for soloing in the mostly busy sonic landscape of Iron Maiden. 'Stranger in a Strange Land' was a fairly successful single at the time, but it would struggle to make its way back into the concert setlist after the *Somewhere in Time* tour. It returned for a brief spell at the start of the 1999 reunion tour, and then finally in all its glory on the 2023 *The Future Past Tour*. In retrospect Adrian Smith must be considered the Man of the Match on this album, and he deserves great credit for making *Somewhere in Time* the classic it is.

'Deja-Vu'

Along with 'Still Life' on *Piece of Mind*, this might be the best track written by Murray, again with melodies and lyrics by Harris. After a deceptively quiet intro with the song's only guitar solo (in this rare case there is no conventional solo in the middle of the song) the track opens into a liberating burst of guitar and vocal melodies of the decisively catchy sort. Harmonies abound, and this is possibly singer Dickinson's finest performance on the album. As the lyrics say, 'You know when you feel deja-vu', but there would be no repeat glory for this song, as it has never been performed live by Iron Maiden.

'Alexander the Great'

Once again, the closing track of an Iron Maiden album is the patented Steve Harris epic, this time in the form of an essay about the ruler of a Greek kingdom in the years 336 to 323 BC. King Alexander III of Macedon, commonly known as Alexander the Great, conquered Egypt and Western

Asia to become one of the most celebrated military commanders in history. This time, in clear contrast to 'Rime of the Ancient Mariner' on the *Powerslave* record, Harris does not seem at all concerned that the lyrics be composed with any regard for breathing space or sensible syntax: 'A Phrygian king had bound a chariot yoke / And Alexander cut the 'Gordian Knot' / And legend said that who untied the knot / He would become the master of Asia.' What would they do without Dickinson?

Musically, 'Alexander the Great' does struggle to live up to the immense legacy of the previous Harris epics, inevitably finding itself in the shadow of 'Mariner' in particular. But there is a welcome variation in the way Harris structures the middle section of the track, opting for a half-time beat over which Smith and Murray solo majestically rather than raising the tempo into a more predictable type of climax. The most remarkable aspect of the song's history is the fact that it was not performed *Somewhere on Tour*, the band instead keeping 'Mariner' in the set and leaving 'Alexander the Great' as the only album epic to that point not to be included on the appropriate tour. In 2023, with the song's long-awaited inclusion in the set for *The Future Past Tour*, Maiden finally broke with tradition for the first time and played a track that had not been featured on the original album tour back in the day.

Related recordings

The *Somewhere in Time* era is also cherished by fans for the quality of the related recordings that would be issued as single B-sides. After the numerous live tracks and original fillers that would be used for their early singles, Iron Maiden had by now developed the routine of recording cover songs for each album project's related singles, 'I've Got the Fire' and 'Cross-Eyed Mary' for the *Piece of Mind* singles, and 'Rainbow's Gold' and 'King of Twilight' for the *Powerslave* singles.

The 'Wasted Years' single was backed with the very pop-oriented 'Reach Out', a song written by Dave Colwell which features Smith on lead vocals. This track signifies where producer Martin Birch felt he should put his foot down, allowing such aesthetics for a single B-side but refusing anything like it to come near the album. The song had been written for a one-off side project that Smith and drummer Nicko McBrain set up in late 1985 called The Entire Population of Hackney, and a further couple of cover songs that Maiden put on their next single would also originate with this side band. The other 'Wasted Years' B-side, 'Sheriff of Huddersfield', is a comedy-parody piece that spoofs the band's manager Rod Smallwood and his adventures when moving to the United States, the music being based on a song called 'Life in the City' by Smith's pre-Maiden band Urchin.

The 'Stranger in a Strange Land' single was backed with Maiden's cover versions of the tracks 'That Girl' (written and subsequently recorded by the band FM) and 'Juanita' (played but unrecorded by the band Marshall Fury), originally performed by The Entire Population of Hackney in 1985. Both songs are well suited to the *Somewhere in Time* sonic aesthetic that the band and Birch created at the time.

LISTENING PREFERENCES

A tell-tale sign of the massive frequency-boosting that happened with Iron Maiden's 1998 CD remasters can be heard on that edition of *Somewhere in Time*: Nicko McBrain's snare drum has a loud and clear reverb on it that seems all new. This high range spaciousness is present in Martin Birch's mix, of course, but on the 1998 remaster it has been pushed right to the front along with every other frequency in the album's dynamic range, resulting in an unpleasant compression of the overall sound. The best sonic representations of the *Somewhere in Time* album, to the author's subjective ears, are the original vinyl and CD editions from 1986, as mastered by George Marino at New York City's Sterling Sound. The sound is also fine on the 2014 heavyweight vinyl edition, but a lack of proper quality control leaves the stereo channels flipped into playing Murray on the right and Smith on the left. The most recent 2015 remaster that is currently available on CD and streaming sounds good, but not on par with the original 1986 editions.

7

Seventh Son of a Seventh Son

Produced by Martin 'Disappearing Armchair' Birch
Released 11 April 1988
Highest chart position and certification at 1/gold (UK), 12/platinum (US)
Featuring Steve Harris (bass), Dave Murray (guitar), Adrian Smith (guitar), Bruce Dickinson (vocals), Nicko McBrain (drums)

Iron Maiden's last album of the 1980s was also the last album of their classic era and the last to feature guitarist Adrian Smith until his return to the band in 1999. Capping a relentlessly prolific decade of recording and touring, Maiden ended this period on a high. *Seventh Son of a Seventh Son* is one of their best and most celebrated albums of all time, and one of a few (besides 1983's *Piece of Mind* and 1995's *The X Factor*) that bassist Steve Harris has often mentioned as among his personal favourite Iron Maiden albums.

After finishing the *Somewhere in Time* tour in Japan in May 1987, the band got together for their next batch of music towards the end of the year. After three projects in a row (from 1983 to 1986) in tax exile, they had now decided to work closer to home. For the writing sessions this meant as close as Steve Harris' rehearsal room on his Essex estate in Sheering near Harlow. Unlike the division between members that marked the writing of *Somewhere in Time*, the *Seventh Son* project took shape around the central idea of a doomed character with paranormal gifts of second sight and had Harris working closely with both Smith and singer Bruce Dickinson in the songwriting. Their first consciously conceptual record, *Seventh Son of a Seventh Son* has eight songs loosely tied together by this theme.

The sonic experimentation that began with the *Somewhere in Time* record is further developed here into what is possibly the most cohesive album the band would ever make. If *Killers* and *The Number of the Beast* were sister records in terms of sound and production, the same could be said for *Piece of Mind* and *Powerslave*. *Seventh Son of a Seventh Son*, in a similar way, has much in common with its predecessor *Somewhere in Time*, chiefly the progressive arrangements of some tracks and the catchy hooks of others. Producer Martin Birch recorded the band at Musicland Studios in Munich, Germany over a period of just a few weeks in February and March 1988, capturing and mixing the warmest and fullest sound of their career. Guitars and synthesizers are blended in a less conspicuous fashion than on the previous record, and Dickinson sounds more engaged on this project.

The musical and conceptual themes of the album are once again translated into truly staggering artworks by illustrator Derek Riggs. Eddie's surreal journey through the 1980s ends here as his torso dissolves into the frozen river or lake on the album cover, Eddie holding out his own heart within which is trapped some tiny creature trying to break free. As if to demonstrate the surplus of creativity, Riggs provides what amounts to a second album cover with the magnificent inner sleeve illustration of Eddie looking in the crystal ball of the prophet. In addition, the single covers for 'Can I Play with Madness', 'The Evil That Men Do' and 'The Clairvoyant' would show bizarre images of Eddie's head, hovering at the very limits of existence, seemingly culminating in sheer paranoid madness with the third eye clairvoyance of the latter. The ethereal beauty of Riggs' artworks captures the spirit and mystique of the album's subject matter, reaching an ultimate point where neither the band nor the illustrator would know where to go next.

However, *Seventh Son of a Seventh Son* was the first Iron Maiden record that took a commercial downturn in the United States of America, album sales slipping from the over 2 million units of *Somewhere in Time* to a still respectable but significantly lower 1.2 million. The tour would also see a declining trend, the days of multiple concerts at venues like the fabled Long Beach Arena now exchanged for mostly single nights at places like the LA Forum. It was now that Maiden had to change from being practically wedded to touring North America, to maintaining their still royal status in Europe while starting to explore other parts of the world more eagerly. The *Seventh Tour of a Seventh Tour* (also profiled as the *Playing with Madness* tour in early publicity) saw Maiden headlining the European 1988 Monsters of Rock concerts, including their first appearance at England's Donington Park.

'MOONCHILD'

Starting out with the haunting strumming of an acoustic guitar and the nursery rhyme of 'Seven deadly sins, seven ways to win', 'Moonchild' is possibly Iron Maiden's most sinister opening track of all time, written by

Adrian Smith and Bruce Dickinson. The blatant heavy metal of its guitar riffs and melodies, draped over busy Harris bass lines and syncopated McBrain drum patterns, is solid proof that it makes no sense to see Smith's subsequent departure from the band as his reaction to the music being too heavy. The synthesizer riff that accompanies the song's accented intro section is a great example of how the late 1980s Iron Maiden could incorporate new elements into their sound while still sounding like no other band or artist than themselves. The obvious opening number for the *Seventh Tour of a Seventh Tour* in 1988, 'Moonchild' would also see successful comebacks, first as an encore on the 2008 *Somewhere Back in Time* tour and then as the opening number again on the 2012–14 *Maiden England* celebration of the *Seventh Son* period.

'Infinite Dreams'

For the first time since 1983, the second track on a new Maiden album is a song that begins slow and quiet. The band had done this to great effect with 'Remember Tomorrow' on *Iron Maiden*, 'Children of the Damned' on *The Number of the Beast*, and 'Revelations' on *Piece of Mind*. 'Infinite Dreams', written by Steve Harris, is as good as any of those, and it imbues the early part of *Seventh Son of a Seventh Son* with a mystical and ethereal vibe that even today transports the listener through space and time in the way that great Maiden songs do.

'Infinite Dreams' was a centrepiece of the *Seventh Son* live set that Maiden took on tour in 1988, but that would be the only time it ever appeared in concert. When Maiden prepared their *Maiden England* show in 2012, the song was dropped from the set during rehearsals, for undisclosed reasons, never to return. Back in 1988, it lent the flow of the concert a serious sense of drama and emotion. It builds through time changes and beautiful vocal melodies and guitar harmonies, ultimately arriving at another iteration of the vaunted Maiden metal shuffle and Dickinson's truly operatic 'Help me, help me to find my true self without seeing the future'. A live version of the song, recorded in Birmingham, England in November 1988, was released as the fourth *Seventh Son*-related single in late 1989, and somewhat inexplicably reached the top 10 in the UK chart despite its length (over 6 minutes) and complexity.

'Can I Play with Madness'

The first single from the album in March 1988, and a British hit at number 3 in the charts (also reaching top 5 positions in Ireland and Norway), 'Can I Play with Madness' started life as an Adrian Smith ballad titled 'On the Wings of Eagles'. Bruce Dickinson thought it could be sped up and turned into something more subversive, depicting a confrontation between the frustrated titular Seventh Son and an older prophet. Steve Harris also chipped in with the song's unconventional middle and solo sections, meaning that the catchy foundations Smith laid down on *Somewhere in Time* is affected here with the quirks and signatures of Dickinson and Harris, to great success. 'Can I Play with Madness', with the three songwriters singing a three-part harmony in the chorus, would show up in the Maiden live set at intervals, in 1988, 1992 (without Smith), 2003–04, 2008, as a surprisingly early second song in the *Maiden England* set in 2012–14, and most recently on *The Future Past Tour* in 2023–24.

'The Evil That Men Do'

Another amalgamation of the Smith/Dickinson/Harris teamwork, 'The Evil That Men Do' is a straightforward heavy rock song that would be issued as the second single from the album in August 1988, replete with a ready-made singalong chorus for the audience. A noteworthy feature of the *Seventh Son of a Seventh Son* album is the fact that the songwriting has not been this integrated between band members since *Piece of Mind*. Further to that, and amazingly, *Seventh Son of a Seventh Son* is this line-up's fourth studio record in five years, in addition to the *Live After Death* double album in 1985. 'The Evil That Men Do', like all other tracks on the album, shows no sign that their productivity is in danger of losing momentum, and it has been the most frequently performed *Seventh Son* track in Maiden's concert sets.

'Seventh Son of a Seventh Son'

Steve Harris turns in first-rate work with the earlier 'Infinite Dreams' and the upcoming 'The Clairvoyant', as well as this title track. To many fans this is the second-best Harris epic of all time, only eclipsed by 'Rime of the Ancient Mariner', and it is even gloomier than its predecessor. Heavy grooves dominate the song's first part, before a darkly quiet middle breakdown leads into a frantic solo section for Murray and Smith, and then a beautiful harmony finish at its tail-end. 'Seventh Son of a Seventh Son' was the resident epic for the *Seventh Son* tour and returned in that capacity for the *Maiden England* tour in 2012–14. More surprisingly, it joined 'Powerslave' and 'Mariner' as the third epic in the set for the fiftieth anniversary *Run for Your Lives* tour in 2025.

'The Prophecy'

In retrospect there is much to be said for Dave Murray's commendable lack of ego. Like 'Deja-Vu' on the previous album, 'The Prophecy' is a top-end Murray composition with Harris lyrics that Maiden never performed on stage. When Murray's music is featured on an album at all, it rarely gets included in the live set. Oscillating between anxious guitar and vocal melodies and muscular riffs reminiscent of Black Sabbath, 'The Prophecy' conveys the desperation of the story's central character as his warnings of disaster go unheeded. The track is eminently listenable for the Murray and Smith guitar work alone, both the acrobatic and the atmospheric, including a breath-taking acoustic coda in folk tradition.

'THE CLAIRVOYANT'
The third single from the album, Harris' 'The Clairvoyant', was released in November 1988 and reached the top 10 of the UK singles chart just in time for the band's triumphant final UK leg of the *Seventh Son* tour. 'The Clairvoyant' was the first song written for *Seventh Son of a Seventh Son* and ruminates on the death of the alleged psychic Doris Stokes in 1987, Harris wondering if she had foreseen her own death and what that kind of foresight would do to the mind of the central character in the *Seventh Son* saga that the band created. The song opens with a catchy major key bass and guitar section and is marked by its audience-friendly galloping chorus, something that ensured its frequent appearances in concert setlists even in the Blaze Bayley era of the mid-1990s.

'ONLY THE GOOD DIE YOUNG'
Possibly the greatest Iron Maiden song never to be performed in concert, 'Only the Good Die Young' is a Harris and Dickinson collaboration that closes *Seventh Son of a Seventh Son* on a ridiculously impressive note. This is essentially an even better track in the style of 'The Evil That Men Do', showcasing excellent guitar and vocal harmonies, as well as properly sinister lyrics that bring the album's theme to a satisfying conclusion. There is even a short bass solo in the song's middle section, and the opening lines of 'Moonchild' are reprised over the strumming of an acoustic guitar as the song and the album signs off.

RELATED RECORDINGS
There were a record four single releases related to the *Seventh Son of a Seventh Son* album, their A-sides and B-sides ranging from original tracks, via a cover and rare re-recordings, to live tracks from two of Maiden's most high-profile performances on their 1988 tour.

The 'Can I Play with Madness' single was backed with an obscure original song by Dickinson and Harris titled 'Black Bart Blues'. The lyrics of the song detail a sordid sexual encounter with a groupie and takes its title from a medieval suit of armour that Dickinson once bought on tour and placed in the lounge of the tour bus. The other B-side on the single is a great-sounding cover of the Thin Lizzy song 'Massacre' from their 1976 album *Johnny the Fox*. At the end of 'Black Bart Blues', in between the two B-side tracks if you are listening to the 12-inch version with both songs, are strange takes of Nicko McBrain fooling around with the drums during recording of *Seventh Son of a Seventh Son* in Munich.

For the 'The Evil That Men Do' single Maiden presented re-recordings of two tracks from their 1980 debut album: 'Prowler '88' and 'Charlotte the Harlot '88'. The songs certainly sound much better in this Martin Birch production, but most fans would probably have preferred that they re-recorded 'Phantom of the Opera' in this way. It was also strange that none of the re-recorded tracks were performed on the 1988 tour, where particularly 'Prowler '88' would have found a welcome spot in the setlist as an encore.

'The Clairvoyant' is a single release where the 12-inch vinyl version is not lifted from the *Seventh Son of a Seventh Son* album. While the 7-inch version has the album track, the 12-inch carries a live recording from Maiden's appearance at the Monsters of Rock festival at Donington Park in August 1988. Confusingly, the accompanying video opted to use the studio recording, even as the footage was from the very same concert performance. Chosen as B-sides were 'The Prisoner (live)' and 'Heaven Can Wait (live)' from the Donington show. The audio was produced by Tony Wilson for the *BBC* radio broadcast and mixed by Martin Birch for Maiden's release. It could be argued that the sound is significantly fatter and fuller than the *Maiden England* recording that would be done later in the tour.

The fourth single from *Seventh Son of a Seventh Son*, and the fourth of them to go top 10 in the United Kingdom chart, 'Infinite Dreams' is another live recording, this time from Maiden's performance at the Birmingham NEC in November 1988. This single was released to tie in with the *Maiden England* concert video in late 1989, and the B-sides 'Killers (live)' and 'Still Life (live)' are very rare outings for deep cuts that were added to the setlist for the closing UK leg of the *Seventh Son* tour. *Maiden England* was a VHS video release, but for some reason not a live album at the time. It would be reissued on DVD, CD, and picture disc vinyl in 2013, making it a proper Iron Maiden live album which is discussed in the live album chapter of part four of this book.

LISTENING PREFERENCES
Like its predecessor *Somewhere in Time* from 1986, *Seventh Son of a Seventh Son* had its greatest audio representation in the original 1988 vinyl and CD editions, of which the represses and reprints from 1989 are equally good to the author's subjective ears. The 2014 heavyweight vinyl edition, cut from the original 1988 master, also sounds very good, while the 1998 CD remaster is predictably hampered by excessive compression and loudness. As before, it should be noted that Iron Maiden albums (in this case

the 2015 digital remaster that is also available on CD) sound good when streamed from a high-quality service through high-quality sound equipment like properly noise-cancelling headphones.

PART TWO
The 1990s

No Prayer for the Dying

Produced by Martin 'The Bishop' Birch
Released 1 October 1990
Highest chart position and certification at 2/gold (UK), 17/gold (US)
Featuring Steve Harris (bass), Dave Murray (guitar), Bruce Dickinson (vocals), Nicko McBrain (drums), Janick Gers (guitar)

Even though 1988's *Seventh Son of a Seventh Son* had enjoyed great reviews and popularity, particularly in Europe and the UK, it seems that the North American sales slump compared to its predecessor *Somewhere in Time* had affected Steve Harris and his band. In what amounts to a reaction to the perceived North American disappointment with Iron Maiden's latest direction, Harris and singer Bruce Dickinson championed a back-to-basics approach for their first album of the 1990s. The songs would be less progressive and more direct, the themes would be less fantastic and more contemporary, and the production would be less sophisticated and more primitive.

A consequence of this redirection was the departure of guitarist Adrian Smith at the beginning of the project in early 1990. The band had intended to write music at Harris' rehearsal room in Essex for three months, before recording in London's Battery Studios in April and May, but they decided to bring in the Rolling Stone Mobile Studio to record as quickly as possible in the rehearsal room in February. Disagreeing with this aesthetic choice and feeling burned out after doing his first solo album, 1989's *Silver and Gold*, Smith left the band. He was immediately replaced by Janick Gers, the former guitarist of White Spirit and Gillan who had also written and recorded with

Dickinson for the singer's first solo record *Tattooed Millionaire*, set for release in May 1990. Martin Birch, working exclusively for Iron Maiden at this point in his career, was called in at short notice to produce the mobile studio sessions before eventually mixing the recordings at Battery Studios in the spring.

No Prayer for the Dying, recorded under the humorous working title *008*, amounted to a radical stylistic departure from Iron Maiden's previous couple of studio albums, with hissing guitars and a snarling Dickinson up front. While the album would become a cult favourite among some hardcore Maiden fans, it would receive a less rapturous critical welcome and see a continuing sales decline in the much-coveted North American market that Maiden had prioritised so highly for many years. Maiden also took their back-to-basics music on the road with a back-to-basics show on the *No Prayer on the Road* tour in 1990 to 1991, toning down the production elements of the 1980s in favour of Marshall stacks and a pyro-free set of old and new material, including only one track from each of their celebrated 1984 to 1988 albums. If this was framed as an artistic attempt to be relevant prior to the great change of Grunge music in the early 1990s, it worked no wonders in commercial terms: *No Prayer for the Dying* did not reignite their career in the United States, where sales dipped below the platinum threshold for the first time since *The Number of the Beast*, although it kept them going in Europe.

The album artwork gives the clear impression that artist Derek Riggs is out of ideas about where to take Eddie, and the image of the Maiden mascot bursting out of a grave is strangely reminiscent of the vastly superior *Live After Death* artwork from 1985. For the single artworks to 'Holy Smoke' and 'Bring Your Daughter ... to the Slaughter', as well as the *No Prayer on the Road* image, Eddie would revert to stalking hellish landscapes and city streets like he did in the early 1980s, and Riggs' role as the exclusive Iron Maiden illustrator was about to come to an end. In many ways, *No Prayer for the Dying* was a watershed in the band's history, the fork in the road where several splits happened and new paths were chosen.

'TAILGUNNER'

Opening the album with ferocious energy, this song by Steve Harris and Bruce Dickinson attempts to vie with *Powerslave*'s 'Aces High' as a dogfighting call to arms, although the lyrics are much more sentimental in their yearning for a bygone hands-on age when bomber planes were flown by people, not computers, and the gunner was made of flesh and blood. 'Tailgunner' (a title Dickinson admitted to having lifted from a porno film) would open the *No Prayer on the Road* set in 1990-91 and was also retained mid-set for the subsequent *Fear of the Dark* tour in 1992.

'Holy Smoke'

Another Harris and Dickinson track, this time attacking hypocritical TV preachers and their money-making schemes, 'Holy Smoke' was picked as the first single from *No Prayer for the Dying* and released in September 1990. The major-key opening riff sounds uncomfortably close to wilfully comical, and despite the infectious energy of the entire band's performances (including Dickinson in venomous form) it is hard to imagine something as unremarkable as this appearing on any of Iron Maiden's albums in the 1980s. The song would never return to the band's concert setlist after the *No Prayer* tour. Janick Gers takes the first solo, followed by Dave Murray, and it is very clear that this guitar duo is different from the Murray/Smith pairing of the 1980s. Gers' style is frantic and much less studied, while his Fender Stratocaster tone is quite similar to Murray's tone on the same type of guitar. Smith often countered Murray with his melodic style and the tones of Gibson Les Paul and Lado and Ibanez, but the Maiden guitar sound of 1990 is less nuanced and significantly poorer.

'No Prayer for the Dying'

The title track is the first, and best, of the album's three songs credited to Steve Harris alone. On the plus side, there are beautiful guitar melodies here, backed up by a tasteful synthesizer arrangement performed by long-time roadie and bass tech Michael Kenney. On the other hand, 'No Prayer for the Dying' unfortunately highlights the record's production issues, chiefly the dry and flat sound of Nicko McBrain's drums. Dickinson stated at the time of the album's release that this song was a particular favourite of his. He even implied a favourable comparison with other quiet-beginning type Maiden songs like 'Hallowed Be Thy Name', 'Children of the Damned', 'Revelations' and 'Infinite Dreams', which in retrospect seems completely absurd. The song was a staple throughout the *No Prayer on the Road* tour but would never reappear.

'Public Enema Number One'

The album continues to be dominated by up-tempo hard rock songs. 'Public Enema Number One' (sorry, this is not a typo, they did switch enemy to enema) is a Dave Murray track with Bruce Dickinson lyrics. Environmental issues were not uncommon in heavy metal lyrics around 1990, and this is Iron Maiden's first contribution of the sort, decrying the wasteful and irresponsible ways of the hippie generation gone wrong. The song was performed early in the *No Prayer* set in 1990–91, but never returned.

'FATES WARNING'
Dave Murray scores his second track on the album, for the first time in his career, with this energetic and catchy song featuring lyrics by Steve Harris. The chorus of 'Be it the Devil or be it Him' is perfectly harmonized in outstanding Dickinson fashion, and a classic-sounding harmony guitar section seals the reputation of 'Fates Warning' as the first of the best two tracks on the album, although Maiden never performed it live. In some ways this is probably the type of Maiden song that people would associate with former guitarist Adrian Smith, a thought that comes to mind with the short breakdown section following the first eminently hummable Gers solo spot on the album. But the credit falls to Murray and Harris this time.

'THE ASSASSIN'
The album's second Steve Harris composition, 'The Assassin' is musically interesting but sorely lacking the appeal of his entries on the previous album, *Seventh Son of a Seventh Son*. The lyrics venture inside the head of a killer for hire who kills for the pleasure and not the money, but the song was dropped from the setlist early in the North American leg of the *No Prayer* tour in January 1991 and was never performed again.

'RUN SILENT, RUN DEEP'
Bruce Dickinson originally wrote these submarine lyrics for the *Somewhere in Time* album, but they were ditched along with his music. When Steve Harris presented this idea for the *No Prayer for the Dying* album, the singer rightly thought that the old lyrics would match. Driven by an excellent Dickinson performance, and highlighted by the mesmerizing melody of the chorus, where the chilling conclusion goes 'Running silent, running deep / Sink into your final sleep', this is the other of the best two tracks on the album. Neither song was ever performed live, but only 'Fates Warning' musters the same Maiden magic as 'Run Silent, Run Deep' of all the songs on *No Prayer for the Dying*.

'HOOKS IN YOU'
The only song that Adrian Smith managed to contribute to before leaving the sessions, 'Hooks in You' is strictly second rate compared with most other songs that he and Bruce Dickinson had previously written together. The track is powered by the band's enthusiastic performance energy, but Dickinson's lyrics about S&M accessories ('Hooks in the ceiling for that well hung feeling') are simply embarrassing, appropriately enough considering the opening line's mention of 'number 22' and its historical connection to

Charlotte the Harlot. The song was dropped for good after the European leg of the *No Prayer* tour in late 1990.

'BRING YOUR DAUGHTER … TO THE SLAUGHTER'

When Iron Maiden were having a much-needed year off from activity in 1989, Bruce Dickinson agreed to write and record a song for the soundtrack to *A Nightmare on Elm Street 5: The Dream Child*. The track, bearing the nasty but tongue-in-cheek title 'Bring Your Daughter … to the Slaughter' was co-written by Dickinson and an uncredited Janick Gers, and led to the recording of Dickinson's first solo album *Tattooed Millionaire*. As it happens, 'Bring Your Daughter' was not featured on that album, because Steve Harris thought it would make a good track to re-record for the next Iron Maiden album.

Taking its stylistic cue from AC/DC and featuring lyrics replete with all the sexualised terror that comes with the slasher movie territory of the *A Nightmare on Elm Street* franchise, the song was released as the second single from the album on Christmas Eve 1990. By issuing a host of different formats for eager fans to buy, Maiden and their management ushered the song to number one in the UK single chart, the only Maiden track ever to reach the top. 'Bring Your Daughter … to the Slaughter' is also the only track from *No Prayer for the Dying* to reappear in concert setlists after the reunion with Dickinson and Smith, but only briefly in the summer of 2003.

'MOTHER RUSSIA'

Steve Harris wrote the words for 'Mother Russia' before he wrote the music, a rare occurrence according to himself. Possibly moved by the series of Eastern European revolutions in 1989 that would culminate in the fall of the Berlin Wall mere days after the release of this Maiden album in October 1990, and the opportunity for democratic progress and freedom in the former Soviet Union, Harris' lyrics lament the history of a great country forever ravaged by war and oppression. Never to be performed live, the sole Harris album epic thus overlooked, 'Mother Russia' is unfortunately the least engaging of this type of Harris song, the intro and coda being the only appealing sections, particularly when the theme is repeated with the full band after the Cossack-inspired verses of the song are past.

RELATED RECORDINGS

Both singles from the album, 'Holy Smoke' and 'Bring Your Daughter … to the Slaughter', featured Maiden versions of cover songs for their B-sides. The former had the band working through 'All in Your Mind' by Stray and 'Kill Me Ce Soir' by Golden Earring, while the latter packed the less obscure 'I'm a Mover' by Free and 'Communication Breakdown' by Led Zeppelin. The tracks are much less remarkable than the B-side covers and originals that graced the singles from the *Somewhere in Time* and *Seventh Son of a Seventh Son* albums.

LISTENING PREFERENCES
Leaving aside the predictably unpleasant 1998 CD remaster, *No Prayer for the Dying* sounds best in its original 1990 vinyl and CD editions, while the 2015 digital remaster, which is also available on CD and heavyweight vinyl, deserves an honourable mention for being faithful to the original mix and master that Martin Birch delivered in 1990. This digital remaster sounds very good when streamed from a high-quality service through high-quality speaker systems or headphones, at least to the author's subjective ears.

9

Fear of the Dark

Produced by Martin 'The Juggler' Birch and Steve Harris
Released 11 May 1992
Highest chart position and certification at 1/gold (UK), 12/none (US)
Featuring Steve Harris (bass), Dave Murray (guitar), Bruce Dickinson (vocals), Nicko McBrain (drums), Janick Gers (guitar)

By the time that Iron Maiden started working on the *Fear of the Dark* album in late 1991, massive changes had swept the world of rock music. Maiden had survived and indeed thrived on the commercial challenge of poppier rock bands like Bon Jovi, Def Leppard and Mötley Crüe in the late 1980s. They had also successfully held their own against the thrash onslaught of Metallica, Slayer, Megadeth and Anthrax. However, the sea change that was signalled by the Guns N' Roses debut album *Appetite for Destruction* in 1987 had by 1991 turned into that band's world-beating double feature *Use Your Illusion I* and *II* alongside Metallica's *Black Album* and Nirvana's *Nevermind*. Ever conscious of the state of the North American market, Maiden now found themselves out-manoeuvred in artistic and commercial terms by the Guns N' Roses and Metallica juggernauts as well as the emerging Grunge rock rebellion of Nirvana, Pearl Jam, Soundgarden and Alice in Chains.

Apparently acknowledging the underwhelming production and performance of 1990s *No Prayer for the Dying*, Steve Harris had converted his Essex rehearsal barn into a proper studio where Iron Maiden would now record their music. Bruce Dickinson, however, was not comfortable with this set-up, deeming it insular and counter-productively self-serving on the part of Harris, who would now co-produce Maiden's music in his own studio at his own millionaire's estate. *Fear of the Dark* would be the last Iron Maiden album overseen by producer Martin Birch before his permanent retirement from the business, and the last until 2000's *Brave New World* where someone other than Harris called the shots in the studio. It would also turn out to be Dickinson's last record with the band until his return in 1999.

Fear of the Dark was the point when new guitarist Janick Gers became an important songwriter for Iron Maiden. He worked in collaboration with both Harris and Dickinson, co-writing the album's lead single 'Be Quick or Be Dead' with the latter. The album is notable for containing a wider variety of rock styles than any other Maiden album before or after, ranging from the AC/DC-inspired singalong of 'From Here to Eternity' to the power ballad-style heartache of 'Wasting Love', songs that would be issued as the second and third singles from the album, respectively. It was also their longest record to that point: Clocking in at almost 58 minutes, it was spread over two vinyl discs in its limited LP edition, while sitting more comfortably on the, by-then commonplace, CD format.

Illustrator Derek Riggs had delivered a sketch for the album cover with a ghostly Eddie at the foot of a terrified person's bed, but the band and manager Rod Smallwood opted for a different artist for the first time in Maiden's career. The chosen artwork saw Eddie as a tree creature in the woods under a full moon, as concocted by Melvyn Grant. The artwork was the template for a recalibrated stage production that built on the economically basic *No Prayer for the Dying* set but featured noticeably more sophisticated lighting designs. Maiden took their new album on tour in the summer of 1992 and immediately experienced the reality of their commercial downturn in North America. The US and Canada leg of the tour was the shortest of their headlining career, and many of the venues were the smallest they had played since the early 1980s. Europe would be a different story, Maiden's status being maintained by a high-profile run as headliners of the 1992 Monsters of Rock tour that included their second top-of-the-bill appearance at Donington Park in England.

Fear of the Dark became Iron Maiden's third chart-topper in the UK, reaching number one in the summer of 1992, although chart positions do not necessarily reflect sustained sales over time. For example, *Fear of The Dark* would chart nearly as high as the 1986 album *Somewhere in Time* in the US, reaching number 12 to the latter's number 11, but it would sell nowhere near the latter's double platinum number of records. As the physical distribution of music came into a steep decline around 2000, chart placement would lose its meaning as a gauge of sales. Simply put, it would take much less in terms of sales to reach the top of the chart when nobody sold much music anymore.

'BE QUICK OR BE DEAD'

The angriest and most closely thrash-related Iron Maiden song of all time, 'Be Quick or Be Dead' was an uncompromising choice for first single. It was released in April 1992 and told the world in no uncertain terms that Maiden meant business as they set out on their *Fear of the Dark* cycle. The fatter and fuller sound of Maiden in 1992, including the tuned-down snare drum of Nicko McBrain, is apparent as this opener bursts forth. Written by Janick Gers and Bruce Dickinson as a scathing attack on predatory capitalism, 'Be Quick or Be Dead' opened the Maiden live set on the *Fear of the Dark* tour in 1992 and 1993. Along with the title track, it is probably the song most responsible for raising Maiden's profile in the summer of 1992 and keeping their European popularity up. Although it would never reappear in concert, it is arguably one of the three strongest songs on the album.

'FROM HERE TO ETERNITY'

The first Steve Harris composition on the record was picked as the second single and released in June 1992. It features the band's fourth reference to Charlotte (following 'Charlotte the Harlot', '22 Acacia Avenue' and 'Hooks in You') and seems to be a paean to the sexual energy of motorcycles. Not quite common as far as Maiden themes go, but then Harris' music is also decidedly non-typical for Maiden on this track, leaning closer to the territory of raunchy rockers AC/DC and thus fitting their type of lyrical innuendoes. 'From Here to Eternity' features a catchy chorus but disappointingly unremarkable verses and solos that leave the impression of a band running low on ideas, although it worked well live.

'AFRAID TO SHOOT STRANGERS'

After the let-down of the previous song, Harris immediately rectifies the situation with 'Afraid to Shoot Strangers', the second of the three best songs on the album and arguably the most Maiden-like of them all. Inspired by the gloomy reality of the First Gulf War in the Middle East in 1990 to 1991, Harris' lyrics take the point of view of a soldier on the battlefield who feels reduced to a military tool and struggles with the notion of firing at and potentially killing other human beings for a cause that is hard to justify.

The slow-burning opening verses build a pensive mood before the staccato mid-tempo hook of the song kicks in, Murray and Gers playing the beautiful melody in unison. When the frantic middle section comes along, in time-honoured Maiden tradition, the guitarists launch into a classic-sounding minor third harmony duet that effectively cements the track as bearing all the hallmarks of the Iron Maiden that fans have come to know and love. 'Afraid to Shoot Strangers' and the title track made a gripping middle point in the *Fear of the Dark* live set, and they are the only two songs on the album that would make appearances on later tours, including the Blaze Bayley era in the mid-1990s. 'Afraid to Shoot Strangers' last appeared in the *Maiden England* set, where it probably replaced 'Infinite Dreams' during rehearsals, in 2012–13.

'Fear Is the Key'

No sooner does the album reach the high point of 'Afraid to Shoot Strangers' before its momentum is stalled again by this subpar Dickinson and Gers collaboration. The riffs and melodies influenced by the Eastern raga scale are somewhat reminiscent of Led Zeppelin's vastly superior 'Kashmir', and Dickinson's lyrical lament about society's sexual fears in the wake of Freddie Mercury's death from AIDS are certainly heartfelt if downbeat. The biggest problem with the song, and possibly the reason why Maiden never attempted to perform it live, is that it lacks a gripping chorus or a dramatic denouement, remaining frustratingly one-note in its presentation.

'Childhood's End'

The middle third of *Fear of the Dark* is now getting bogged down in unrealised song ideas that would have been inconceivable on Iron Maiden albums of the 1980s. 'Childhood's End' is an environmentally conscious Harris song that is built almost exclusively on the F#m – A – E – D chord progression. On any previous record this would have been considered filler material if included at all, but it seems that the extension of playing time that comes with the CD format encourages Maiden to include tracks that would have been edited out in the vinyl era of the 1980s. This is unfortunate, as the comparatively stronger first and last thirds of the album lose their impact in the presence of too many musically uninteresting songs.

'Wasting Love'

Another Gers and Dickinson collaboration, 'Wasting Love' was originally conceived for the latter's *Tattooed Millionaire* solo album in 1990, but eventually found its home on *Fear of the Dark* as the first proper Iron Maiden ballad since 'Prodigal Son' on *Killers* back in 1981. The track was released as the third single from the album in September 1992, albeit only in European territories, and was nowhere near a hit. The most interesting characteristic of the song is Dickinson's lyrical ponderings about relationships and dishonesty, just prior to his departure from Maiden. He muses about maybe one day being 'an honest man', seemingly regretting that up until now he is simply 'doing the best I can'. 'Wasting Love' is a deliberate change of pace and a stylistic novelty in the Iron Maiden catalogue, but it is still a poor track in light of the band's best efforts.

'THE FUGITIVE'
Taking full advantage of the more muscular drum sound that Harris and Birch created for the *Fear of the Dark* album, 'The Fugitive' is a Harris track that could have fallen through completely if not for the sonics. Nicko McBrain's thundering toms in the song's opening section is the chief attraction of an otherwise forgettable tune that tells of a lonely person being hunted for a crime they did not commit. Dickinson's raspy and aggressive vocal style, which came into being with *Tattooed Millionaire* and *No Prayer for the Dying* in 1990, seems uncomfortably out of sync with the melancholy lyrics, and the listener gets the uneasy feeling that the song material and the singer's performance style are not a good match.

'CHAINS OF MISERY'
The album's first track by Dave Murray is written in collaboration with Bruce Dickinson, and chugs along in a slow shuffle that never manages to raise much interest. It is another poor song on what amounts to Iron Maiden's least cohesive record so far, its only saving grace being an exceptionally uplifting Murray guitar solo that brings on the goosebumps.

'THE APPARITION'
Coming out of the weakest middle section of any Iron Maiden album to this point, 'The Apparition' launches the album's final third in frighteningly poor fashion: with a resounding thud. Written by Gers and Harris, this exploration of Harris' thoughts about paranormal phenomena is lyrically fascinating but musically impotent. As much as we can be sure that any Maiden song on any Maiden album has its own share of fans, it is impossible for the author to give a favourable objective assessment of the merits of 'The Apparition'.

'JUDAS BE MY GUIDE'
And then, what a contrast. This is the last of the three best songs on the album, following 'Be Quick or Be Dead' and 'Afraid to Shoot Strangers'. Written by Murray and Dickinson in collaboration, 'Judas Be My Guide' would not have been musically out of place on *Somewhere in Time* or *Seventh Son of a Seventh Son*. Short and to the point in a way that would become more and more rare for Maiden as the years went by, there radiates from this song a pure joy of performing catchy heavy metal. Again, Dickinson sounds best when he edges back towards the clean tone of his previous style in the 1980s, and the crowning glory of the song is his double-tracked harmony vocals in the chorus.

'WEEKEND WARRIOR'

And just like that, the album comes crashing down again with another subpar song that defies objective assessment. Sounding inexplicably like Harris and Gers trying to write a song for Dickinson's *Tattooed Millionaire* hard rock pastiche, ripping off AC/DC at their least compelling, 'Weekend Warrior' moralizes about the culture of football hooliganism in the UK. As such, the track points ahead to the unfortunate football themes of Maiden's 1998 *Virtual XI* album package and is a clear sign of a band losing their teeth in the early 1990s. Despite making obvious efforts to branch out of an increasingly unpopular horror and fantasy niche that rock critics were chaining them to at the time, it is inescapable that Iron Maiden are most convincing when they sound utterly like themselves. The stylistic diversification exemplified by several of the *Fear of the Dark* songs amounts to nothing more than imitating other classic rock bands, and Maiden now seems to have lost the creative touch of their 1980s period. They do, however, have one more bullet left in their gun.

'FEAR OF THE DARK'

Despite its haunting quiet intro, featuring a beautiful guitar melody played by Janick Gers, 'Fear of the Dark' is not as good as the three best songs on the album. In fact, the main riff that kicks in after the intro is utterly infantile, and most of the song is made up of uninspired chord progressions draped over a Maiden-by-the-numbers gallop. But none of the author's criticism matters: 'Fear of the Dark' would steadily climb its way to the top of the tree as the most popular Iron Maiden title track of all time, and it is currently surpassed only by 'Run to the Hills' and 'The Trooper' as the most played Maiden song on Spotify.

One needs only to witness Iron Maiden live to realise what a concert phenomenon this Steve Harris track has become. No other song, no matter the setlist, gets a response that equals the pandemonium that greets 'Fear of the Dark'. The song has been present on every single tour since 1992, with the sole (and logical) exception of the 2005 *Early Days* tour that focused on the 1980–83 period of the band. Protests were heard, loud and clear, and 'Fear of the Dark' was consequently featured as an out-of-period anachronism in the band's period recreations in 2008 (*Powerslave* era) and 2012 (*Seventh Son of a Seventh Son* era).

Ultimately, there is no denying that Maiden suffered a dearth of inspiration in the wake of Adrian Smith's departure. Years later, Steve Harris would reflect that, 'maybe Maiden lost something when Adrian left.' It could be argued that they lost something essential, for Iron Maiden have never made a truly great record without Smith. At the time of *Fear of the Dark*, the title track's live power and the ferocious energy of 'Be Quick or Be Dead' kept their momentum up despite disappointing North American showings, but times were now changing quickly, and Maiden would soon be looking for a new singer.

RELATED RECORDINGS

The B-side of the 'Be Quick or Be Dead' single featured an original blues number credited to the entire band, 'Nodding Donkey Blues', and a cover of the 1973 Montrose song 'Space Station No. 5'. Furthermore, the previous 1986 B-side 'Sheriff of Huddersfield' got a kind of sequel in the unlisted hidden track 'Bayswater Ain't a Bad Place to Be', where Bruce Dickinson once again mocked and parodied manager Rod Smallwood, this time over the simple accompaniment of Janick Gers' acoustic guitar.

A much more interesting set of B-sides were allocated for the next two singles, the first of which was 'From Here to Eternity'. Apart from the cover of Budgie's 1975 song 'I Can't See My Feelings' and Chuck Berry's 1956 hit 'Roll Over Beethoven' repurposed as an homage to Harris' long-time roadie and handyman Vic Vella, titled 'Roll Over Vic Vella', there are finally more live recordings to savour. Maiden had recorded their appearance at London's Wembley Arena on the *No Prayer for the Dying* tour in December 1990, and two tracks are presented on this single: 'Public Enema Number One (live)' and 'No Prayer for the Dying (live)'. These tracks are interesting for any fan or critic as they mark the first proper live recordings of Iron Maiden post-Smith with Gers as the new guitarist. The latter track in particular features a phenomenal vocal performance from Dickinson.

The third single from *Fear of the Dark*, 'Wasting Love', appearing as a so-called radio edit shorn of almost 1 minute of its running time, presents a further three tracks from Wembley 1990 as B-sides: 'Tailgunner (live)', Holy Smoke (live)' and 'The Assassin (live)', all of which benefit from the band's Gers-inspired high energy and particularly Dickinson's impressive high range. 'Hooks in You (live)' from Wembley 1990 would be featured on the subsequent 'Fear of the Dark (live)' single in 1993, meaning that only 'Bring Your Daughter … to the Slaughter' has not been released of the seven *No Prayer* songs included in Maiden's 1990 live set. This entire show is obviously safe in the band's vault and available for any potential future deluxe editions. In the wake of *Fear of the Dark*, however, Steve Harris decided to open the floodgates in terms of live album releases, and these are discussed in the book's part four.

LISTENING PREFERENCES

The original CD edition of *Fear of the Dark* from 1992 still sounds as good as the album ever did, and it should be noted that the 2015 digital remaster that is currently available on both CD and heavyweight vinyl also sounds fresh and dynamic. The 1992 vinyl edition was strictly limited and has become a sought-after collector's item. The 1998 CD remaster, however, is once again the least pleasant listening experience of any editions of the album.

10

The X Factor

Produced by Steve Harris and Nigel Green
Released 2 October 1995
Highest chart position and certification at 8/silver (UK), 147/none (US)
Featuring Steve Harris (bass), Dave Murray (guitar), Nicko McBrain (drums), Janick Gers (guitar), Blaze Bayley (vocals)

Two years after the traumatic departure of Bruce Dickinson in 1993, Iron Maiden returned with their new singer Blaze Bayley, formerly a founding member of the British hard rock band Wolfsbane. Dickinson had opted to leave a Maiden that he felt had lost their creativity and that failed to engage his own urges for artistic explorations. He would eventually record and release the albums *Balls to Picasso* (1994) and *Skunkworks* (1996) while Maiden faced the world with their new singer and their long-awaited new album, *The X Factor*.

Bayley had auditioned for Iron Maiden in late 1993, beating several other singers to secure the job. In January 1994, Maiden gathered at Steve Harris' Barnyard Studios in Essex, the rehearsal barn turned into a recording studio, to start writing and rehearsing material for a new album. In the much less commercially successful decade of the 1990s, working in what amounted to a glorified home studio was certainly a way to save money. Furthermore, Harris had invested his own money in setting up the Barnyard, and like Dickinson said, 'the band were gonna pay him back for using his studio.' The work of creating *The X Factor* was easily the most drawn-out album process of Maiden's entire career. Where an album like *The Number of the Beast* (1982) had been recorded and mixed in a matter of five weeks, and even the sonically sophisticated *Somewhere in Time* (1986) had taken no more than nine months from start of rehearsals to release, the first Maiden album with Bayley would take an unprecedented eighteen months to write and record, a period reaching from early 1994 into the late summer of 1995.

With the absolute retirement of Martin Birch, producer of all Maiden albums in the period from 1981 to 1992, Steve Harris decided to produce Maiden himself. Manager Rod Smallwood was not comfortable with this decision, sensing that a more objective set of ears was fundamental in the process of recording and mixing music. As a sort of compromise, Nigel Green was brought in as Harris' co-producer. Green, who had worked alongside Birch as an engineer on *Killers* in 1981 and *The Number of the Beast* in 1982, seems to have been little more than an in-house studio engineer on *The X Factor*, all creative direction and decision-making apparently resting on Harris' shoulders. The result of this was a dark and brooding Iron Maiden album, with a dry and primitive sound, where most songs started with quiet intros and the band (presumably under Harris' direction) almost completely avoided catchy choruses and their trademark harmonies for guitars and vocals.

The visual aspect of the new Iron Maiden album also saw a major change, with Eddie no longer appearing in a painting but as a grotesquely lifelike silicone sculpture captured in a photograph. Although the flat photo used for the album cover can easily be mistaken for a detailed illustration, the angled photo used for the 'Man on the Edge' single cover gives a better impression of the photo-realistic Eddie model that was designed and sculpted by Hugh Syme. Maiden had liked Syme's work on the Megadeth albums *Countdown to Extinction* (1992) and *Youthanasia* (1994) and wanted an equally realistic development for Eddie.

All these changes added up to a new chapter in Iron Maiden's history that would be considerably less celebrated than their 1980s heyday. *The X Factor* received the band's least generous reviews since *Killers*, and the album sold less and charted lower than any Maiden album before it, particularly in North America. The band, including Bayley, would in later years defend this Maiden period by pointing out the general downturn in the popularity of classic heavy metal in the mid-1990s as well as the generally declining sales of physical media. However, this defensive explanation side-steps the fact that CD sales were at an all-time high in the mid-1990s, and it conveniently ignores the reality that heavy metal bands like Metallica and Pantera were selling huge amounts of records at the time. In truth, the declining fortunes of Iron Maiden cannot be attributed to anything but the fact that fans and critics alike were less enamoured with the new Maiden than the old. Iron Maiden themselves valiantly battled on through their 1995–96 *The X Factour* but were greeted with the smallest audiences of their headlining career almost everywhere they went, a clear signal that the changes in line-up and production aesthetics were not well received.

'SIGN OF THE CROSS'

This new era in Iron Maiden's history opens with a song that is not only the best of the period, but one that would not have been inferior on any earlier Maiden album either. 'Sign of the Cross' is an 11-minute Steve Harris epic, refreshingly opening rather than closing the album, and it is one of the two Blaze Bayley era tracks that Maiden would revisit on several tours in the post-Bayley period, the other being the next album's centrepiece 'The Clansman'. 'Sign of the Cross' is easily Maiden's most atmospheric opening song since 'Moonchild' on *Seventh Son of a Seventh Son* in 1988.

Inspired by the religious doubts and dilemmas of the 1980 Umberto Eco novel *The Name of the Rose* and its 1986 film adaptation, 'Sign of the Cross' is a suitably dark introduction to an album that is filled with the melancholy, depression, and despair of Steve Harris at his lowest personal ebb, following his divorce and Dickinson's departure from Maiden. The song opens with an ominous Gregorian chant and quiet bass and guitar lines, as Bayley intones 'Eleven saintly shrouded men, silhouettes stand against the sky'. Building through a time-honoured Maiden gallop into a dramatic breakdown and all-out glorious heavy metal climax, 'Sign of the Cross' wins the listener over. The immediate impression of Bayley is that he possesses a more limited range than Dickinson but makes up for it with sheer determination. Two worrying aspects are however apparent. First, Bayley tends to stray out of tune sometimes, occasionally pitching too sharp. And second, Harris' and Green's production is light on guitars, their faint hiss completely overwhelmed by the comparatively very loud drums.

'LORD OF THE FLIES'

The worrying production elements of the album unfortunately get exacerbated as the record unfolds. 'Lord of the Flies', a Janick Gers and Steve Harris collaboration that seems lyrically inspired by the 1954 William Golding novel and film adaptations thereof, features a surprisingly poppy chorus but is also the album's first clear instance of under-production that gets in the way of the music's potential. Bayley's lower range makes him struggle to reach the energy level that could lift the track (Dickinson would tellingly pitch it an octave higher when he performed it live) and the lack of a proper vocal production with suitable harmony backing leaves him exposed. There is no reverb or double tracking that might have eased the singer's performance, but Gers thankfully alleviates the problem somewhat with a gently affecting guitar solo and melody section. 'Lord of the Flies' was released as the second single from *The X Factor* in February 1996, and it was revisited with the subsequent Dickinson and Smith line-up on their *Dance of Death* tour in 2003–04.

'Man on the Edge'

Released as a single ahead of the album in September 1995, 'Man on the Edge' was Blaze Bayley's first songwriting contribution to Iron Maiden, the result of a writing session between himself and Janick Gers in the latter's home studio in early 1994. Bayley's lyrics were inspired by the 1993 thriller *Falling Down*, starring Michael Douglas as the frustrated ordinary man that turns to violence, while Gers' music was reminiscent of his work on the previous album's 'Be Quick or Be Dead' opening track. After first considering the lengthy 'Sign of the Cross' and then the quietly catchy 'Lord of the Flies', Harris decided that 'Man on the Edge' would be the lead single from *The X Factor*. The track and its vocal performance would be a feather in Bayley's cap, and the song was even retained in the setlist for a short tour after Dickinson's return to the band in 1999. Even though it is musically unremarkable, it is the only immediate and up-tempo track on the entire album.

'Fortunes of War'

The second of several gloomy Steve Harris epics on the album, 'Fortunes of War' is much less appealing than 'Sign of the Cross'. It is also the point on the album where the listener might start to wonder where Maiden's patented harmony aesthetic has gone. After a quiet intro and a slow build into that well-known Maiden gallop, the wordless melodic chant that crowns the track comes without a hint of harmony layering in either the vocals or guitars. Much like the absence of any reverb or other processing of Bayley's voice, it must be a conscious choice on Harris' part to steer clear of the guitar harmonies that are so much a hallmark of his band's musical identity. This could be from a fear of sweetening the sonics of a track that revels in the darkness and depression of war as a metaphor for any kind of life challenge, but ultimately it makes the track less triumphant than a better production could have made it. 'Fortunes of War' was performed throughout 1995–96 but was retired from the live set after the first concert of Maiden's 1998 tour for the *Virtual XI* album.

'Look for the Truth'

Another track by Bayley and Gers, this time with some added input from Harris, 'Look for the Truth' recalls 'Lord of the Flies' in that it is a potentially catchy tune which unfortunately loses its impact because the production does not grant it backing vocals that could layer melodic singalong harmonies, neither in the chorus nor in the wordless chant that gets repeated throughout. There is also a regrettable lack of powerful guitars, although Murray's part of the solo section does feature a brief flurry of harmony notes that reminds listeners of which band they are listening to. Another bleak tale of depression and anxiety, 'Look for the Truth' is one of the few songs from *The X Factor* that were never performed on tour.

'The Aftermath'

Coming so closely on the heels of 'Fortunes of War', 'The Aftermath' feels redundant both in its slow-to-fast structure and in its lyrics about the senseless sacrifice of soldiers in war. Since Maiden recorded more songs than they needed for *The X Factor*, and three of them were relegated to B-sides, it seems a bad call not to drop one of these and rather keep the superior 'Justice of the Peace' that never made the album. 'The Aftermath' was featured on *The X Factour* in 1995–96 and then dropped from live sets permanently, but it is also notable as one of Bayley's finest vocal performances in his time with Maiden.

'Judgement of Heaven'

Another one of the few *The X Factor* tracks never to be performed live, this Harris composition is one of the best songs on the album. It is another excursion into the darkness of personal doubts and depressions, ostensibly fuelled by Harris' divorce and the split with Dickinson, this time going as far as admitting that 'I've felt like suicide a dozen times or more'. Quickly resolving that such a way out is the easy way, that 'The hardest part is to get on with your life', the song is chillingly honest and graced with some of the most uplifting melodies on the album. Another great plus with 'Judgement of Heaven' is the middle section where we finally hear that long-anticipated minor third harmony from Murray and Gers. A more generous vocal production could have lifted the track further, but Bayley is consigned to a dry and flat soundscape that does him no favours.

'Blood on the World's Hands'

Steve Harris' concern for the state of modern society grew ever clearer throughout the 1990s, and 'Blood on the World's Hands' rips into this theme with apparently carefree abandon. His words are harsh, his doom is merciless, Harris acting like a lord meting out a sentence upon the world in retribution for his own sense of dark helplessness and despair. Perhaps this emotion was ever the inevitable outcome of the dark journey that is *The X Factor*, but in this instance the restless riffs and vocals of the music are less memorable than they were on the preceding track. 'Blood on the World's Hands' was performed on *The X Factour*, but never appeared in a setlist again after that.

There is no doubt that *The X Factor* is heartfelt, but as the album reaches its final lap there is equally little doubt that Maiden now lack too many crucial ingredients: more diverse songwriters, a more sophisticated guitarist, a more able singer, and a producer and studio with the skills and facilities to capture these intentions and emotions in a better way. There had never been a Maiden album where Harris was so clearly in charge, producing their music in his own studio, and a listener's enjoyment of *The X Factor* will probably depend on the degree to which they are satisfied or frustrated with over one hour of music from this very dark place.

'THE EDGE OF DARKNESS'
'The Edge of Darkness' was one of the several B-sides issued with first single 'Man on the Edge', and it could be assumed that the band felt the song to be somewhat representative of the album in a way that the A-side certainly is not. Coming this late in the album's running order, 'The Edge of Darkness' is another quiet-beginning type of song that ultimately loses impact due to the sheer amount of similar music ahead of it. Written by Harris, Bayley and Gers in conjunction, it is one of the three most solid tracks on the album, along with 'Sign of the Cross' and 'Judgement of Heaven'. Apparently inspired by Joseph Conrad's 1899 novella *Heart of Darkness* and its liberal and contemporary adaptation into Francis Ford Coppola's classic film *Apocalypse Now* from 1979, it builds through a staccato beat reminiscent of the previous Maiden album's 'Afraid to Shoot Strangers' and into a more up-tempo middle section awash with Murray and Gers solos and melodies, Murray's part again including a brief burst of his patented harmony notes. The song would be retired from concert performances at the conclusion of *The X Factour* in 1996.

'2 A.M.'
A track that should clearly have been left off the album, '2 A.M.' is a depressive dirge, both by design and by accident. The lyrical subject matter is, once again, a bleak state of personal depression, this time about the failure to find meaning in either work-life or private life and wondering how to leave it all behind. The lyrics are written by Bayley, while the unappealing music is credited to Gers and Harris. Thankfully, the track was never performed in concert, although it is sure to have its share of fans that will disagree with the author about its merits.

'THE UNBELIEVER'
At least 'The Unbeliever' takes to task the gloomy outlook of the preceding ten tracks in an apparent attempt at critical self-reflection. Asking the hard questions about whether we are in fact afraid of what we find if we take an honest look inside, the song functions as a kind of resolution to the

dark catharsis of *The X Factor*. Composed by Harris and Gers, most of the track is musically unremarkable, with a strong exception for the glorious chorus over which Bayley nearly screams the words, and the ethereal middle section with its beautiful guitar melody. Perhaps not surprisingly, given its somewhat intricate time signatures and the middle section's crucial double-tracking of McBrain's toms, 'The Unbeliever' is the fourth track on *The X Factor* that would never be given a chance on stage in front of an audience.

RELATED RECORDINGS

Iron Maiden spent about eighteen months writing, recording, and mixing *The X Factor*. One result of this extensive time frame for working was the creation of more songs than needed for the album, a first in Maiden's recording history. A total of fourteen original songs were recorded, plus two cover versions designated for single B-sides. The different formats of first single 'Man on the Edge' featured all three of the leftover original songs. The worst of these is the overbearing 'I Live My Way' credited to Harris, Bayley and Gers. 'Judgement Day', written by Gers and Bayley, is better but was dropped possibly due to its uncomfortable similarity to the previous album's lead single 'Be Quick or Be Dead'. The best of the bunch is Dave Murray's only songwriting contribution to this album project, 'Justice of the Peace'. It is up-tempo and catchy and features both guitar and vocal harmonies that were in very short supply on *The X Factor*. In fact, the song's chorus holds the single instance of harmony vocals that Bayley recorded for the entire project, as incredible as that sounds. The song's lyrics, written by Harris and decrying the rise of crime in society in a quite tabloid fashion, are possibly not a seamless fit for *The X Factor*, but neither was 'Man on the Edge' really. The song would have been a benefit to an album that comes off as sorely monotonous.

For the B-side of second single 'Lord of the Flies', Maiden recorded The Who's 'My Generation' (from their 1965 debut album) and UFO's 'Doctor Doctor' (from their 1974 album *Phenomenon*). The original version of the latter is well known to Maiden fans as the final background track to precede the start of every Maiden show.

LISTENING PREFERENCES

Interestingly, *The X Factor* seems to fit better into a double vinyl album format, which can be appreciated with the recent 2 LP heavyweight reissue, possibly because grouping the tracks into twos or threes makes the totality of the record's 71 minutes less overwhelming. In this format *The X Factor* splits neatly into four episodes, and the 2015 digital remaster that the current vinyl edition is taken from sounds very good on both vinyl and CD. However, to the author's subjective ears, the original 1995 CD edition is still the best-sounding version of the album available, and many fans and connoisseurs also praise the now very expensive collector's item that is the 1995 clear vinyl 2 LP limited edition.

11

Virtual XI

Produced by Steve Harris and Nigel Green
Released 23 March 1998
Highest chart position and certification at 16/silver (UK), 124/none (US)
Featuring Steve Harris (bass), Dave Murray (guitar), Nicko McBrain (drums), Janick Gers (guitar), Blaze Bayley (vocals)

Singer Blaze Bayley had felt that the making of *The X Factor* dragged on interminably, but he would feel that the making of his second album with Iron Maiden went by too fast. Written and recorded in the latter half of 1997, after an extended break that only saw them add the new track 'Virus' to the 1996 *Best of the Beast* compilation, *Virtual XI* was the sound of a happier and more settled band, but one that now released albums that were far behind their competition in terms of sonic and compositional quality. Visually speaking, the cover artwork by artist Melvyn Grant, who had previously created the *Fear of the Dark* artwork, also proved one of the least popular and engaging incarnations of the band's Eddie (pictured here as some kind of virtual reality demon) and signalled a poorly conceived music, computers and football crossover that plagued their album and tour in 1998.

A team's starting line-up in football (known as soccer in the US) has 11 players, and this was Maiden's eleventh record. The band's management were also overseeing Maiden's upcoming computer game at the time, and all these interests coalesced in the *Virtual XI* album title that made little sense to most people. Like its predecessor, *Virtual XI* was recorded in Steve Harris' own Barnyard Studios in Essex, England. The production was again headed by Harris in conjunction with Nigel Green, and the songwriting was also more heavily Harris-dominated than it had been since Maiden's earliest days. In short, Harris now had more control over Iron Maiden's direction and aesthetics than at any other point in the band's history, and yet it bears reminding that the departures of guitarist Adrian Smith, singer Bruce Dickinson, and producer Martin Birch, all three leaving the fold over the course of the years 1990 to 1993, had not been according to Harris' wishes. Bayley's songwriting contributions were down from five to three tracks compared to the previous album, while guitarist Janick Gers was down from a personal high of seven co-writes on *The X Factor* to a bewildering one single co-write on *Virtual XI*, leaving most of the work in Harris' lap.

Virtual XI would see Iron Maiden's poorest record sales since the beginning of their career, even as global CD sales were hitting a historic high point at the end of the 1990s. There was also a growing concern behind the scenes about Bayley's lack of ability to sing much of the band's classic catalogue on stage. The *Virtual XI* world tour in 1998 made it clear that Maiden's star had fallen dramatically in North America, the UK and Europe, while they could still co-draw large crowds in South America as part of multi-band bills. By the end of 1998, manager Rod Smallwood had facilitated a major rethink of Maiden's line-up, and Bruce Dickinson (who had by then re-engaged his metal instincts with the Adrian Smith-assisted albums *Accident of Birth* in 1997 and *The Chemical Wedding* in 1998) would return to replace Blaze Bayley. Although Bayley would bemoan the loss of an opportunity to write and record a third album with Maiden, arguing that it could have turned things around for them, it is hard to envision what this line-up of Maiden could potentially have achieved beyond *Virtual XI*.

'FUTUREAL'

The last instance of Steve Harris writing a short and direct song for Iron Maiden, 'Futureal' is 3 minutes of catchy riffs and melodies, one of two great tracks on the album along with 'The Clansman'. Times have certainly changed since then, as three or four tracks like this would fit into the running time of each of Harris' songs on Maiden's latest album *Senjutsu*. However, all is not well: the bewildering lack of harmony guitars continues to grate on the listener, as though Harris stubbornly does not want to acknowledge a sonic hallmark of classic Maiden. Tellingly, Blaze Bayley, who authored the 'Futureal' lyrics about being trapped in virtual reality, included a live version in his later solo set where his band played minor third harmonies in the main riff of the song. A blistering Dave Murray guitar solo thankfully does incorporate harmony notes. But another disturbance is the lack of depth to the production, midrange-heavy drums and guitars fighting for space alongside Bayley's dry and reverb-less vocals. 'Futureal' was issued as the second single from the album in July 1998, and was the opening song for the *Virtual XI* tour. More surprisingly, it was retained for the band's reunion tour with Dickinson in 1999.

'THE ANGEL AND THE GAMBLER'
Released as the first single from the album in March 1998, against the advice of manager Rod Smallwood, 'The Angel and the Gambler' was met with disbelief by many fans at the time. A decidedly primitive rock and roll tune inspired by The Who's 1971 classic 'Won't Get Fooled Again', it was drawn out to the length of nearly 10 minutes, much of that playing time being filled with Bayley intoning 'Don't you think I'm a saviour? / Don't you think I could save you? / Don't you think I could save your life?' eight times in the song's middle section and then another incredible ten times in the final chorus. Composed by Harris, the song is severely blighted by inexplicable production choices like the synthesized brass stabs in the intro and the lack of care taken to make sure Bayley does not pitch too sharp. 'The Angel and the Gambler' was performed nightly on the *Virtual XI* tour but has never since been revisited.

There exists a public misconception that the Blaze Bayley albums of Iron Maiden have been underrated. In fact, this is claimed so often, and the albums are praised for being hidden gems in so many published articles and internet stories, that they cannot truly be underrated. Quite the reverse, it could be argued that they are overrated. Some Maiden fans will insist that *Virtual XI* is a great album, which is certainly a fair opinion to hold. The author's opinion does not align with this, but such disagreements do not make the album underrated.

'LIGHTNING STRIKES TWICE'
The album's first of several songs with a quiet beginning, 'Lightning Strikes Twice' is co-written by Dave Murray and Steve Harris. After a build-up through a rare 3/4 waltz beat, the song explodes into a riff that is reminiscent of 'Sanctuary' many years earlier. An entertaining entry for Maiden fans, perhaps, but the weak production robs the song of its potential thunder and lightning, and it is yet another track that would have been well served by third or fifth harmony guitars in the melody section that follows the solos. 'Lightning Strikes Twice' was featured on the 1998 tour and then permanently dropped.

'THE CLANSMAN'
The undisputed highlight of *Virtual XI* is this Harris composition inspired by the Mel Gibson film *Braveheart* from 1995, about the First War of Scottish Independence around the year 1300. Creating a musical landscape to go with the image of the Scottish Highlands and its windswept hills, 'The

Clansman' marks the point when Harris' obsession with Celtic melodies and chord progressions took hold, an aesthetic that would influence nearly every song he would write for Maiden on his own from this point onward. The triumphant chorus of 'Freedom!' has the first instance of harmony vocals to be heard on a Maiden album since the arrival of Blaze Bayley.

'The Clansman' was retained in the Iron Maiden concert setlist following the *Virtual XI* tour, featuring in both the subsequent tours with Dickinson in 1999 and 2000–01. Thus, it was also included on the *Rock in Rio* live album that was recorded in Brazil in 2001. It was then revisited for a short summer tour in 2003 before being a popular feature on the *Legacy of the Beast* tour in the period from 2018 to 2022, and thereby immortalised again on the *Nights of the Dead* live album that was recorded in Mexico in 2019. Next to the previous album's 'Sign of the Cross', which was also immortalised on those very same live records, 'The Clansman' has become the most highly rated song from the Bayley era of Iron Maiden by fans and critics alike.

'WHEN TWO WORLDS COLLIDE'

A straight-ahead and unremarkable heavy rock song, 'When Two Worlds Collide' was co-written by Murray, Bayley, and Harris. The lyrics tell a tale of disaster movie proportions, a celestial body on a collision course with Earth, but they also work as a metaphor for all kinds of conflicts of interest that we experience in life, and particularly the great change in Bayley's own life when he went from being 'Blaze Bayley of Wolfsbane to Blaze Bayley of Iron Maiden', as the singer himself once put it. 'When Two Worlds Collide' was featured in the *Virtual XI* live set in 1998 and then permanently retired.

'THE EDUCATED FOOL'

Harris keeps up his prolific songwriting contribution to *Virtual XI* with a second Celtic-tinged track to accompany 'The Clansman'. 'The Educated Fool' is not as strong, but it is a fascinating trip into the life philosophy of Harris as he approaches middle age. The lyrics discuss his feelings about growing older and having less sure answers for anything in life. The recent passing of Harris' father seems to have triggered a new sense of humble maturity in the band leader's outlook, having four kids of his own (at the time) and three younger sisters that he felt an ever-stronger obligation to. The contrast to the vitriol and darkness of Harris' lyrics on the previous album is remarkable, those sentiments being replaced here by a softer sense of melancholy and uncertainty.

Musically there are many compelling things about 'The Educated Fool', ranging from the beautiful melodies of the quiet intro via a stomping verse and into a glorious chorus that sports the second instance of harmony vocals on the album. However, it is impossible to ignore the production issues that make a promising song fall short, and the notion of how much better 'The Educated Fool' would have been with the production and performances that the next line-up of Maiden would deliver on *Brave New World* in 2000. This is another of the songs that was performed on the 1998 tour, but never since then.

'Don't Look to the Eyes of a Stranger'
Another Harris composition of epic length, at over 8 minutes, this song pales in comparison with the previous track and particularly 'The Clansman'. Any promise of appeal is severely impeded by the quiet middle section where Bayley intones 'Don't look to, don't look to, don't look to the eyes of a stranger' a mind-blowing twenty times, before the song disintegrates into parody with the rabid up-tempo section of guitar melodies and solos.

Another public misconception about this era of Iron Maiden, one that is regularly promoted by both Harris and Bayley, is that these records were the start of Maiden getting more progressive. This is unfortunately an absurd statement about a band that had previously recorded *Seventh Son of a Seventh Son* (1988) and that counted 'Hallowed Be Thy Name', 'Revelations' and 'Rime of the Ancient Mariner' (to name but a few tracks) among their celebrated output of decidedly progressive-sounding songs through the years. *The X Factor* is not a progressive rock record just because it has an overabundance of long songs on it, and it would be more on point to argue that *Virtual XI* was the beginning of Harris' fascination with Celtic melodies and the Em—C—G—D chord progression, although the latter is admittedly not a feature of this particular track.

'Como Estais Amigos'
The only track on the album where Harris does not write or co-write the music, 'Como Estais Amigos' sees the only *Virtual XI* writing credit for guitarist Janick Gers. It is not one of his better compositional efforts, but there is enough emotional impact in the middle section and Gers' solo, as well as the Bayley lyrics that lament the 1982 Falklands War and its repercussions of animosity, to argue that the album ends on a note that sums up the era: well-intentioned, but frustratingly shorn of production values and artistic hallmarks like the third or fifth Maiden harmony guitar section, which does not appear even once on the entire album. The guitar tones of Murray and Gers on their Stratocasters are not easily distinguishable from each other, and so the sonic landscape becomes flat in comparison to Maiden's signature 1980s works. The Bayley line-up signs off on this melancholy and disappointing note, but things would soon be very different for Maiden and their fans.

Related recordings

The B-sides of the *Virtual XI* singles, 'The Angel and the Gambler' and 'Futureal', consisted of live tracks recorded on tour for *The X Factor*. Taken from the band's 1 November 1995 gig at a relatively small venue in Gothenburg, Sweden (Spotify claims this to be the huge Ullevi Stadium if you stream the tracks from the *Best of the B-sides* compilation, which is utterly false), both old and new songs are presented as performed by the Bayley line-up. New songs include 'Blood on the World's Hands', 'The Aftermath' and 'Man on the Edge' from *The X Factor*, while Bayley also tries his hand at 'The Evil That Men Do' from *Seventh Son of a Seventh Son* and the more singer-friendly 'Afraid to Shoot Strangers' from *Fear of the Dark* (the latter included as a video). This entire show is obviously archived and could potentially be released at some point.

The song 'Virus' is not really related to the production of *Virtual XI*, but it should be mentioned here. At the end of *The X Factour* in September 1996, Iron Maiden released their first compilation, titled *Best of the Beast*. Included on all the formats was a new song that Maiden had written and recorded that summer. 'Virus' is rare, in that Harris, Gers, Murray and Bayley are all listed as co-writers. An awkward and prolonged quiet intro, punctuated by bursts of accents, eventually gives way to the song proper: a catchy guitar melody leads into a verse of accusations against critics, and then a triumphant chorus that features in-short-supply harmony vocals that help Bayley sound stronger. The sign of a more confident band, enjoying the energy of touring for the first time in two years, the song unfortunately bodes less well in terms of production, as it sounds very much like a precursor to *Virtual XI*.

Listening preferences

Virtual XI is a rare example of a remaster being preferable to the original release, at least to the author's subjective ears. The original 1998 CD mastering was always quite loud and unpleasant, not helpful to the problematic mix of the album, but this has been alleviated to some degree with the 2015 digital remaster which is also available on CD and heavyweight vinyl. Maybe this new processing inevitably makes the album more listenable, but a suspicion could also be raised that Bayley's tendency to pitch a little sharp has been reined in by a delicate touch of digital tuning. At least to the author, the vocals sound better on the remastered version of this album in a way that seems to go beyond a question of dynamic range or loudness. This version is in any case softer and more comfortable on the ears, and in the author's opinion it is clearly the best way to experience the album.

PART THREE

The 2000s and Beyond

12

Brave New World

Produced by Kevin Shirley, co-produced by Steve Harris
Released 29 May 2000
Highest chart position and certification at 7/gold (UK), 39/none (US)
Featuring Steve Harris (bass), Dave Murray (guitar), Nicko McBrain (drums), Janick Gers (guitar), Bruce Dickinson (vocals), Adrian Smith (guitar)

A better title for Iron Maiden's 2000 comeback album with singer Bruce Dickinson and guitarist Adrian Smith could not be imagined. It signals a triumphant return, but also a glorious new era. Dickinson and Steve Harris had been in complete agreement about several things when they met in late 1998 to discuss their possible reunion: a new producer was needed, a state-of-the-art studio would be sought, Smith should be invited back, and Maiden would look ahead to the future instead of back in nostalgia. This commitment to going forward and creating something new was underlined by Harris' insistence that Janick Gers would stay with the band in a three-guitar six-man line-up. Dickinson and Smith effectively put their other careers and projects on hold to recommit themselves one hundred percent to making Iron Maiden great again. After taking their first tentative steps in rehearsal in the spring of 1999, which included writing some of the material that would go on the album, Iron Maiden did a relatively short tour of Europe and North America from early July through September that seemingly consolidated the new line-up easily and exhibited a surprisingly strong vibe between Harris and Dickinson. *Brave New World* indeed.

Taking the proper time and care in early 1999 to sift through candidates for the job of producer, Maiden decided on Kevin Shirley, previously known for his work with the likes of Aerosmith, Dream Theater, Silverchair and The Black Crowes, among others. Shirley suggested that Maiden try to work in a way they had not done since *Killers* in 1981, setting the entire band up in the studio to play live in the room together and work up tracks from there. A reluctant Harris agreed to give it a go, and subsequently never wanted to work any other way. *Brave New World* was recorded in Studio Guillaume Tell in Paris, France in late 1999, and it signalled a major shift and a clear improvement in Maiden's sonic production values. Starting with this album and developing further over subsequent projects in the years to come, Shirley was able to build something of a bridge between the traditionalist philosophy of Harris and the ambitious and sometimes radical aesthetics of Dickinson and Smith. Fans would inevitably have diverging opinions on the merit of the sound of Maiden's albums with Shirley, but the band's longevity and creativity into their sunset days must undoubtedly be partially credited to Shirley's facilitation.

Brave New World was a critical and commercial comeback for Iron Maiden, with fan interest also picking up noticeably as the *Brave New World Tour* in 2000 saw them headline venues like London's Earls Court Arena, Stockholm's Olympic Stadium, and New York City's Madison Square Garden, all a very far cry from any of their tours in the 1990s. Although the art of album packaging would be less important to the band in this new age than it had been in the 1980s, their original illustrator and Eddie inventor Derek Riggs even made a surprising return to deliver the Eddie in the sky over the futuristic cityscape of digital artist Steve Stone. Most importantly, though, the thunderous yet contemplative music of Maiden's new album seemed to inspire not just a familiar feeling for older fans, but to create that very important breed: a new generation of Iron Maiden fans. It is not without flaws, but *Brave New World* has rightfully gained the status of classic album in Iron Maiden's catalogue.

'THE WICKER MAN'

This was the first track that the reformed 1999 line-up of Iron Maiden worked on together in rehearsal, the first new piece of music that saw the band feeling their way towards what would be the new Maiden. Opening with a catchy Adrian Smith guitar riff and thundering accents on Nicko McBrain's toms, it is hard to tell that this is the same band that ended their disappointing previous studio album just two years earlier with the lacklustre 'Como Estais Amigos'. Apart from the fact that singer Bruce Dickinson sounds immediately at home replacing his own replacement Blaze

Bayley, there is a world of difference in the sonic qualities of Kevin Shirley's production. As much as some fans would always bemoan the absence of Martin Birch (long since retired and never in the frame for this project), it is hard to overstate the lift in production values that Maiden experienced from 1998 to 2000.

Released as the first single from the album in early May 2000, the track was chiefly written by Smith, lyrics and melodies were added by Dickinson, and the singalong chant at the end was a patented Steve Harris contribution. The lyrics might be some of Maiden's most defiantly uplifting and life-affirming of all time, telling you to be ready for when the hand of fate moves your way, and to realise that 'every second is a new spark that sets the universe aflame'. With its kick-drum-driven chorus in half-time and Dickinson's promise that 'Your time will come' soaring over the top, 'The Wicker Man' was always an obvious stage song. It opened the 2000–01 *Brave New World Tour* and returned to the set in 2010–11 and 2018–19.

'Ghost of the Navigator'
This is a tale about navigating the seas of life, told from the point of view of a person who knows not where they are but only where they have been. The quest is to avoid distraction and temptation and to find the path through the storm. Built on music written by Janick Gers in collaboration with Harris, and with trademark Dickinson melodies and lyrics putting the proper fantastic spin on it, 'Ghost of the Navigator' was a solid live track in the 2000–01 set, and it returned on the 2010 leg of Maiden's *The Final Frontier* tour.

'Brave New World'
Just after re-joining the band in early 1999, Dickinson suggested that a good title for their new album together would be *Brave New World*. As the title stuck, Dickinson set about writing lyrics based on Aldous Huxley's classic 1932 novel of the same name. The music was written by Dave Murray in collaboration with Harris, and in many ways this is the track that seals the triumph of the reunited Maiden. After a hauntingly beautiful quiet intro, there is a restrained power in the first full-band verse that transcends anything Maiden had done before, a melancholy melody coupled with a maturity of strength that needs no showing off. The chorus might be a Maiden gallop by numbers and a tad repetitive, but it was ready-made for audience participation in a way that made it a great feature on the 2000–01 tour. It even stayed in the set for the subsequent 2003–04 *Dance of Death* tour, and it reappeared on the 2010 *The Final Frontier* leg where the band focused heavily on their post-2000 output.

The debut album, *Iron Maiden* in 1980, was a surprise hit that featured classics like 'Running Free' and 'Phantom of the Opera'. (*Artwork by Derek Riggs*)

Killers in 1981, the first album produced by Martin Birch, featured classics like 'Wrathchild' and 'Killers'. (*Concept by Dave Lights; artwork by Derek Riggs*)

The breakthrough album *The Number of the Beast* in 1982, Bruce Dickinson's first record with the band, featured the hit single 'Run to the Hills' and the fan favourite 'Hallowed Be Thy Name'. (*Concept by Rod Smallwood; artwork by Derek Riggs*)

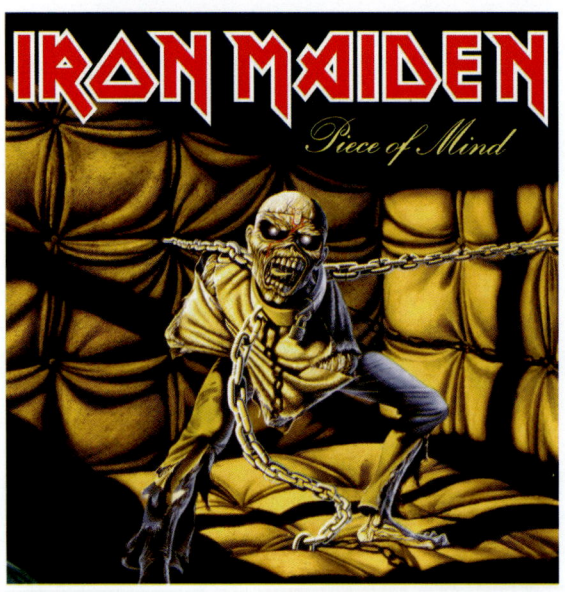

Piece of Mind in 1983 was a milestone for Iron Maiden, particularly in North America where they toured as headliners for the first time, and it included celebrated classics like 'Revelations' and 'The Trooper'. (*Concept by Iron Maiden, Rod Smallwood and Derek Riggs; artwork by Derek Riggs*)

The height of Maiden's classic era, the *Powerslave* album in 1984 featured timeless classics like '2 Minutes to Midnight' and 'Rime of the Ancient Mariner'. (*Concept by Iron Maiden, Rod Smallwood and Derek Riggs; artwork by Derek Riggs*)

Somewhere in Time in 1986, with one of the most celebrated incarnations of Eddie travelling through space and time, included the popular single 'Wasted Years' as well as the more obscure epic 'Alexander the Great'. (*Concept by Rod Smallwood and Derek Riggs; artwork by Derek Riggs*)

The last album of Iron Maiden's classic era, *Seventh Son of a Seventh Son* in 1988 featured all-time greatest Maiden songs like 'Infinite Dreams' and 'Only the Good Die Young', as well as many that are more well-known. (*Concept by Bruce Dickinson, Rod Smallwood and Derek Riggs; artwork by Derek Riggs*)

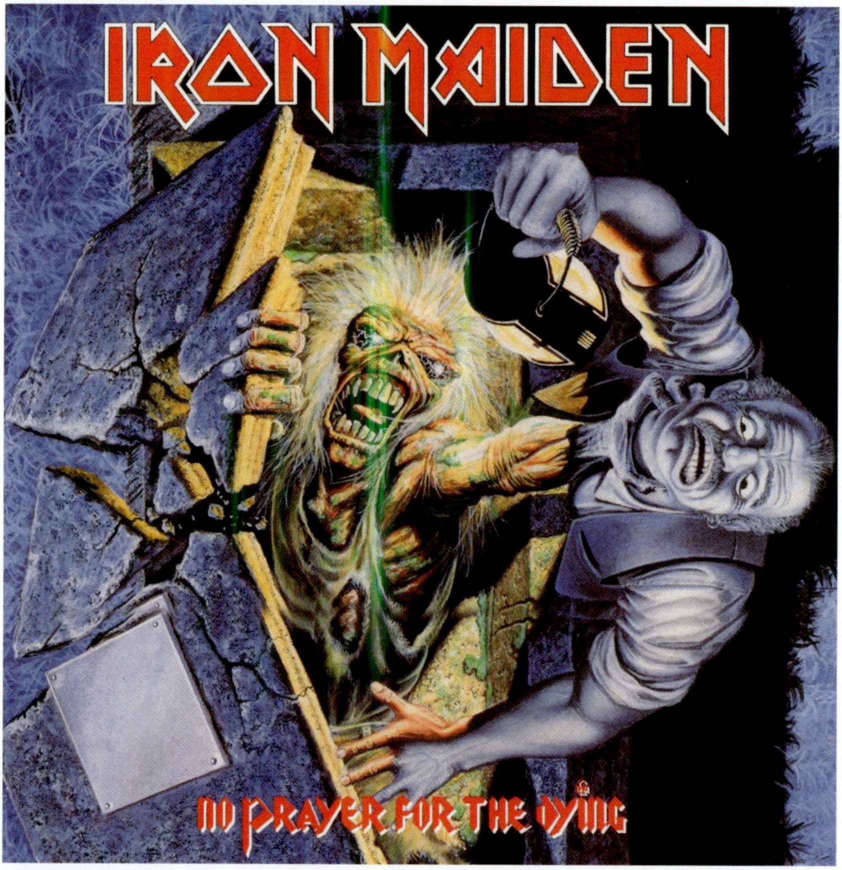

No Prayer for the Dying in 1990, when Maiden swapped Adrian Smith for Janick Gers, included the hit 'Bring Your Daughter … to the Slaughter'. (*Artwork by Derek Riggs*)

One of Maiden's highest charters, *Fear of the Dark* in 1992, featured 'Be Quick or Be Dead' and the band's most popular title track of all time, 'Fear of the Dark'. (*Artwork by Melvyn Grant*)

A new era began with *The X Factor* in 1995, the first album with Blaze Bayley. Produced by Steve Harris and Nigel Green, it included the milestone track 'Sign of the Cross'. (*Artwork by Hugh Syme*)

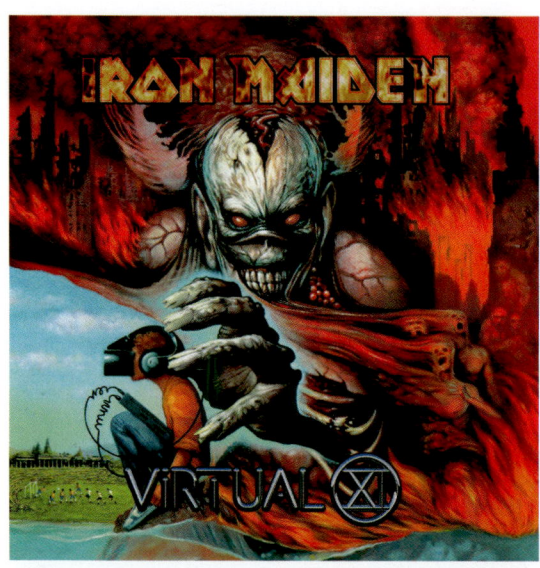

Virtual XI in 1998 was Blaze Bayley's last album with Maiden, and it included another milestone track in the form of 'The Clansman'. (*Artwork by Melvyn Grant*)

Bruce Dickinson and Adrian Smith returned for the triumphant *Brave New World* in 2000, the first album produced by Kevin Shirley. It featured milestone tracks like 'The Wicker Man' and 'Blood Brothers'. (*Concept by Peacock; artwork by Derek Riggs and Steve Stone*)

Dance of Death in 2003 consolidated Maiden's return to prominence and featured the milestone tracks 'Paschendale' and 'Journeyman'. (*Proof of concept preliminary artwork by David Patchett*)

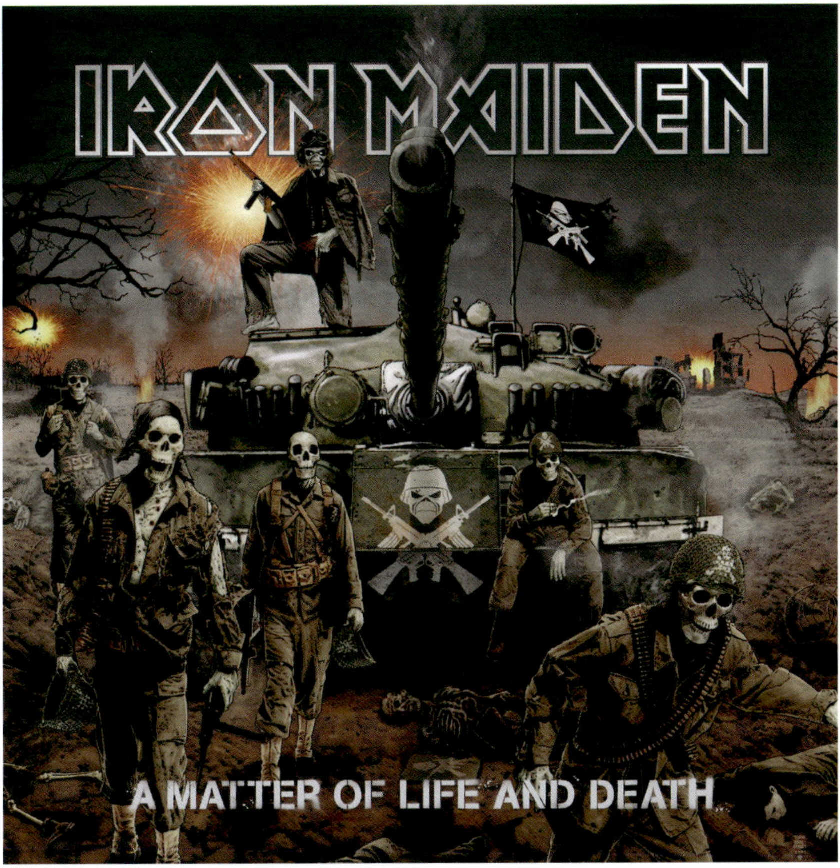

A modern Maiden masterpiece, *A Matter of Life and Death* in 2006 featured tracks like 'Brighter Than a Thousand Suns' and 'For the Greater Good of God'. (*Artwork by Tim Bradstreet with Grant Goleash*)

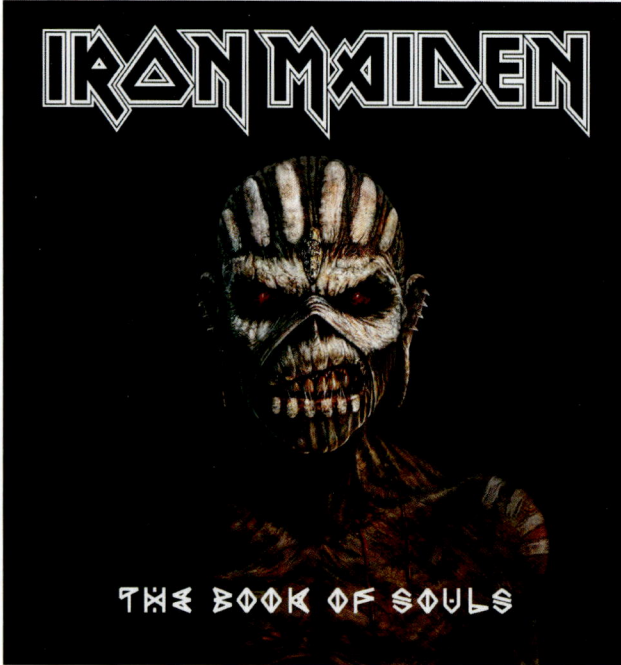

Above: *The Final Frontier* in 2010 included the milestone tracks 'Coming Home' and 'The Talisman'. (*Artwork by Melvyn Grant*)

Left: *The Book of Souls* in 2015 featured two Dickinson songs as its bookends, the sinister 'If Eternity Should Fail' and the 18-minute mini-symphony 'Empire of the Clouds'. (*Artwork by Mark Wilkinson*)

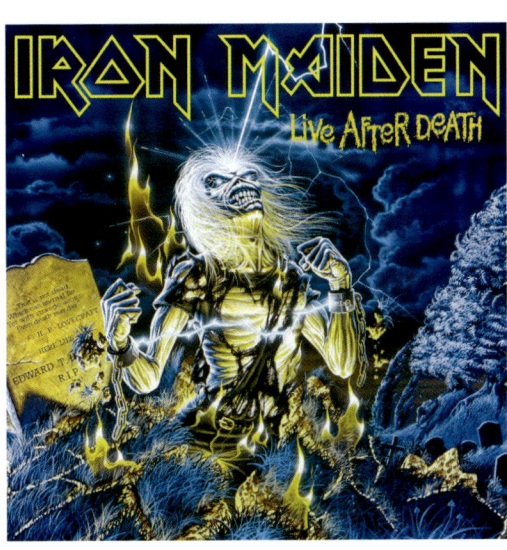

Senjutsu in 2021 was Iron Maiden's seventeenth studio album in a career that now spans fifty years. It is also the sixth album featuring the current line-up in their more than twenty-five years of being reunited and expanded. Milestone tracks include 'The Writing on the Wall' and 'Hell on Earth'. (*Concept by Steve Harris; artwork by Mark Wilkinson with Michael Knowland*)

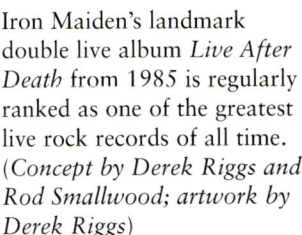

Iron Maiden's landmark double live album *Live After Death* from 1985 is regularly ranked as one of the greatest live rock records of all time. (*Concept by Derek Riggs and Rod Smallwood; artwork by Derek Riggs*)

Maiden England was released as a concert video in 1989. The feature would be reissued as a live album and DVD in 2013 to accompany Iron Maiden's period-oriented *Maiden England* world tour. (*Artwork by Derek Riggs*)

The 2002 release of the *Rock in Rio* live album and DVD celebrated the return of a stronger and more exciting Iron Maiden in the new millennium. (*Concept and artwork by Peacock; photography by Mick Hutson and Dean Karr*)

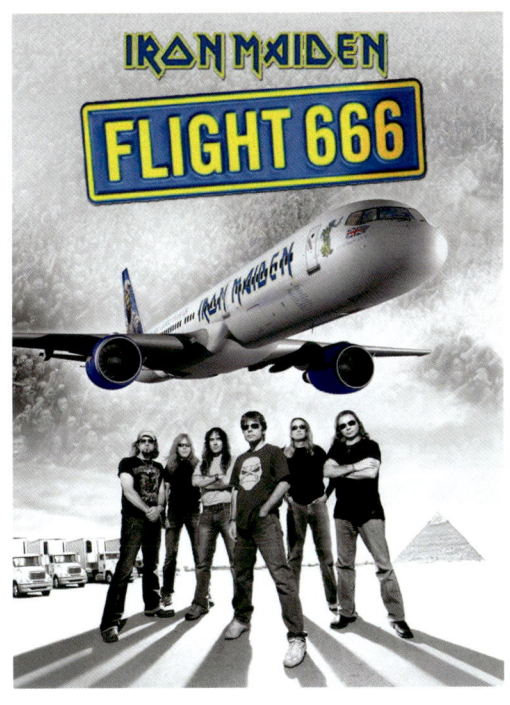

Above: The 2005 live album and subsequent DVD *Death on the Road* consolidated the longevity and creativity of Iron Maiden after the return of Bruce Dickinson and Adrian Smith. (*Artwork by Melvyn Grant*)

Right: Iron Maiden's hugely successful world tour in 2008–09, dubbed *Somewhere Back in Time*, was saved for posterity by the impressive combo of a documentary feature, a concert film, and a live album, all titled *Flight 666*. Posing on the cover is the longest-serving line-up of Iron Maiden: Adrian Smith, Janick Gers, Steve Harris, Bruce Dickinson, Nicko McBrain, Dave Murray. (*Photography by John McMurtrie*)

En Vivo! in 2012 was Iron Maiden's fourth and final concert album and video that was produced and mixed by Kevin Shirley. (*Artwork by Melvyn Grant, Daniel Reed and Peacock; photography by John McMurtrie*)

Left: Iron Maiden released their first compilation album, *Best of the Beast*, in 1996. (*Artwork by Derek Riggs*)

Opposite below: Iron Maiden live in 1980, left to right: Dave Murray, Paul Di'Anno, Clive Burr, Steve Harris, Dennis Stratton.

Iron Maiden live in 1985 on the monumental *Powerslave* tour: Bruce Dickinson and Steve Harris at the front of the stage.

Above: Iron Maiden live in 1988 on the *Seventh Son of a Seventh Son* tour: Steve Harris, Bruce Dickinson and Dave Murray throw their hands up to the sky.

Left: Blaze Bayley replaced Bruce Dickinson at the end of 1993 and stayed until Dickinson agreed to return at the end of 1998. This is Blaze live on the *Virtual XI* tour in 1998.

Opposite below: Iron Maiden at the peak of their powers, live on the 2008 *Somewhere Back in Time* tour: Adrian Smith, Steve Harris, Dave Murray, Janick Gers.

Adrian Smith and Bruce Dickinson have been pivotal in the history of Steve Harris' life's work, both in the 1980s and after their return in 1999.

Another triumphant return for Iron Maiden, live on stage in 2016 on their *The Book of Souls* tour, a year after Dickinson had beaten throat and neck cancer.

Bruce Dickinson looks back to the future, on Iron Maiden's *The Future Past* tour in 2023. The set focused on material from their latest album *Senjutsu*, and (to the fans' delight) their classic 1986 record *Somewhere in Time*.

'Blood Brothers'

The only song on the album credited solely to Harris, the band chief now preferring to write in conjunction with other band members, 'Blood Brothers' caps the strong first third of *Brave New World* in perfect fashion. A folk-inspired track in a waltz beat, with plenty of Harris' early Jethro Tull influences coming through, 'Blood Brothers' is one of the most successful examples of the bassist's preoccupation with Celtic melody. Harris claims to have been working on this track for a while, dating back to Blaze Bayley's time in the band, but it was never completed or seriously considered for inclusion on the previous album.

The song was partly inspired by the passing of Harris' father, but its lyrics and catchy melodies would make it universal in its appeal, and therefore a strong live number for the band. It was performed throughout the *Brave New World Tour* in 2000–01, and revisited in 2010, 2016–17, and on the final leg of the *Legacy of the Beast* tour in 2022.

'The Mercenary'

The first track on the album that was clearly an idea left over from the time of *Virtual XI*, 'The Mercenary' tellingly does not come close to matching the previous four songs. Generic and unexciting, this Gers and Harris composition pales in comparison to the opening third of the record and launches the problematic second third that ruins the momentum of *Brave New World*. It was performed on the 2000–01 tour but never since revisited.

'Dream of Mirrors'

A favourite with critics at the time of the album's release, this overlong Gers and Harris track about blurry lines between dream and reality is another entry that Smith later stated had been left over from the previous era of Maiden. Former singer Bayley also claims to have written some of the lyrics for the song, without being credited, and 'Dream of Mirrors' might not have sounded out of place on any of the previous two Bayley-era Maiden albums, except for the fact that it is impossible to imagine Bayley singing it. Much like 'The Mercenary', it leaves something to be desired when compared to the album's opening salvo of four tracks that were immediately fresh and appealing. It was retired following the 2000–01 tour.

By this point of the album, two things become clear. First, the new line-up of Maiden can clearly come up with better and more inventive material than the band did in its previous incarnation. Second, the reason for Gers' one single writing credit on *Virtual XI*, its closing ballad 'Como Estais Amigos', might be that two more of his tracks never made it far enough in development to be recorded, namely 'The Mercenary' and 'Dream of Mirrors'.

'THE FALLEN ANGEL'

Still struggling to pick up the pace again, 'The Fallen Angel' features music by Smith, only his second entry on the album, and lyrics and melodies by Harris. It is a short and heavy song with the kind of shuffle beat that was common for Maiden in their early years, and it sports one of the few choruses on the album where Dickinson layers harmonies. Yet it lacks punch and appeal compared to 'The Wicker Man', and it was only attempted in concert for a very few shows in January 2001.

'THE NOMAD'

One of only two songs on the album never to be performed live, Murray and Harris' 'The Nomad' is another track that Smith has stated was left over from the *Virtual XI* writing sessions in 1997. Unlike 'The Mercenary' and 'Dream of Mirrors', however, 'The Nomad' actually sounds like a fresh idea with its Persian scale riffs, and it is utterly impossible to imagine Bayley singing it the way Dickinson does. This song would later find controversy with a plagiarism lawsuit that claimed its half-time middle section was lifted from Beckett's early 1970s song 'Life's Shadow', as was also the case with some lyrics in Maiden's 'Hallowed Be Thy Name'. In any case, this prolonged middle part of the song, with traditional guitar solos stepping aside for ethereal guitar melodies to have space, is its best feature.

'OUT OF THE SILENT PLANET'

This track was released as the second single from the album in October 2000. Unusually, this was a song that the band had not performed on the tour at all, and it would only be attempted at a few concerts in January 2001, like 'The Fallen Angel'. Written in collaboration between Gers, Dickinson, and Harris, 'Out of the Silent Planet' is a catchy but somewhat unrealized track with lyrics inspired by the 1956 science fiction film *Forbidden Planet*. Following 'The Nomad' it ensures that the final third of the album sits a notch or two above the middle section.

'THE THIN LINE BETWEEN LOVE AND HATE'

The final song on the album is perhaps its greatest surprise and an entry most resilient to the test of time, although Maiden never performed it on stage. A slow-burning number by Murray and Harris, featuring patented philosophical what-does-it-all-mean lyrics from the band leader, 'The Thin Line Between Love and Hate' bursts with delicate and catchy melodies that would oddly not have been unfit for U2. The two versions of the chorus are delights to the ears and the heart, the first version being a multi-tracked low-register Dickinson harmony piece while the second sees him soaring into the upper register in that way that brings goosebumps. When this second version is finally also augmented by harmonies, the return of Dickinson to Maiden seems like just what the universe needed to come back into balance. When you think the song is finally winding down, it starts back up again with a coda of beautiful guitar and bass melodies. It's like Iron Maiden want to assure you that they still have a long way to go.

Related recordings
The single releases for *Brave New World* featured a host of live tracks recorded on the previous year's *Ed Hunter* reunion tour. 'The Wicker Man' carried 'Futureal' and 'Man on the Edge' mixed by Kevin Shirley, and 'Powerslave' and 'Killers' mixed by front-of-house engineer Doug Hall. There was also an alternative mix of 'The Wicker Man' made available for radio play, with more lines of vocals in the chorus than the album version, a sort of question-and-answer type of arrangement where Dickinson responds to 'Your time will come' with 'Thy will be done' and a few other bits and pieces. It is frankly a little baffling and aimless, and nothing but a YouTube curiosity these days.

'Out of the Silent Planet' carried more live tracks from 1999, 'Aces High' mixed by Hall, and 'Wasted Years' mixed by Shirley. In an apparent attempt to achieve airplay, 'Out of the Silent Planet' itself is presented here as an edit that leaves out the pointless guitar-noodle intro and condenses the track into a slightly more sensible form at just over 4 minutes rather than just over 6. The entirety of Maiden's 2000–01 *Brave New World* set would of course be captured for posterity on the *Rock in Rio* live album and DVD, both of which are discussed in part four of this book.

Listening preferences
Brave New World is one of the rare Iron Maiden albums that were mastered for their original release by the legendary George Marino at New York City's Sterling Sound. He had previously mastered some classic Maiden albums in the 1983–88 period, and Shirley seems to have mixed the record with a view to precisely this type of highly professional mastering, something that would be vetoed by Harris for later albums. Consequently, *Brave New World*

sounds great in its original 2000 CD release. It is also good as the later 2015 digital remaster that is currently available on CD and vinyl as well as streaming, and thus one of the few Maiden albums where you cannot really go wrong no matter what version you listen to.

13

Dance of Death

Produced by Kevin Shirley, co-produced by Steve Harris
Released 8 September 2003
Highest chart position and certification at 2/gold (UK), 18/none (US)
Featuring Steve Harris (bass), Dave Murray (guitar), Nicko McBrain (drums), Janick Gers (guitar), Bruce Dickinson (vocals), Adrian Smith (guitar)

If anyone thought that Iron Maiden's massive comeback in 2000 had been a cynical one-off cash-grab, they were wrong. Where *Brave New World* was the album that reignited Maiden's flame, *Dance of Death* was the one that made it clear they were in it for the long haul. The album was written at the end of 2002 and recorded in London's Sarm West Studios in early 2003 with producer Kevin Shirley once again at the helm.

After the *Brave New World Tour* in 2000–01 and the release of the *Rock in Rio* live album and DVD, bassist and band leader Steve Harris insisted on an extended hiatus to recharge batteries. When Iron Maiden re-emerged in 2003, the first order of business was a summer tour of Europe and North America, leading up to the new album's release in September. The band debuted 'Wildest Dreams' in the set, but the rest of their new music had to wait until the proper *Dance of Death* tour rolled out in October. After another leg around Europe, the band moved on to South America, North America, and Japan in early 2004. The excitement might not have been on par with what they had experienced on the previous tour, but the new show was visually and musically interesting and would be captured for posterity with the *Death on the Road* live album in 2005 and an accompanying concert DVD in 2006.

In defence of illustrator David Patchett, he had submitted the *Dance of Death* cover piece as a proof of concept but was blind-sided when the band decided to use it as it was. Patchett could possibly have turned it into a great bit of artwork, but using the decidedly unfinished version is one of the many baffling visual decisions of Maiden's later career. Commercially speaking, *Dance of Death* saw Maiden's charting positions continue to climb while actual album sales began a post-2000 downturn that would go on for decades.

'Wildest Dreams'
The energy of 'Wildest Dreams' is admirable for a band that had by this point moved well into their middle age, but the musical content is far less inspiring than the previous album's opener 'The Wicker Man'. Written by Adrian Smith and Steve Harris, the song was performed pre-release on the 2003 summer tour and issued as the album's first single some days ahead of the album in September. It would be the opening number on Maiden's 2003–04 *Dance of Death* tour and also reappeared on the 2010 leg of *The Final Frontier* tour.

'Rainmaker'
Much better than the opener, this collaboration between Dave Murray, Bruce Dickinson and Steve Harris is a punchy and melodic rocker that exhibits some fine guitar work in the areas of riffs, power chords, leads and harmonies alike. It slots into place among the many life-affirming Iron Maiden tunes of all time, welcoming the cleansing rain so that 'the cracks in our lives, like the cracks upon the ground, they are sealed and are now washed away.' Released as the album's second single in November 2003, the song was featured on the *Dance of Death* tour in 2003–04 but was then permanently retired.

'No More Lies'
In what is fast becoming a formulaic pattern, here is a quiet intro that builds into a Steve Harris epic with plenty of the Celtic-tinged guitar melodies he by now applies to every track he writes on his own. 'No More Lies' was issued as a souvenir EP in March 2004 after the end of the tour. An unexciting entry in the *Dance of Death* live setlist, the track nonetheless returned for the post-2000 focus of the 2010 *The Final Frontier* tour.

'Montségur'
On the other hand is 'Montségur', one of the strongest songs on the album but one that has never been performed live. Written by Janick Gers in

collaboration with Dickinson and Harris, the opening riff is possibly Maiden's heaviest ever, and a strong vocal performance combined with delicate guitar harmonies in the track's middle section elevates this to the higher tier of *Dance of Death* songs. The lyrics portray the horrific siege and massacre of the titular Cathar stronghold in 1244, a late coda to Pope Innocent III's Albigensian Crusade to eliminate Catharism (an opposition to the Catholic Church) in southern France, and Maiden create the soundtrack like only they can.

'Dance of Death'

Gers and Harris also worked together to create the album's spellbinding title track. The guitarist was inspired to write the piece after viewing Ingmar Bergman's classic film *The Seventh Seal* from 1957, and the bassist turned it into a folkloric campfire story 'to chill the bones', as the lyrics say. Carried by another top-notch vocal performance from the inimitable Dickinson, the song would become a centrepiece of the show on the *Dance of Death* tour and would subsequently be featured in Maiden's *The Final Frontier* set in 2010–11. 'Dance of Death' marks the point in time when Gers truly emerged as a key songwriter of epic Iron Maiden songs in the later years of their career.

'Gates of Tomorrow'

Dance of Death oscillates frustratingly between some of Iron Maiden's best ever music and utterly forgettable filler material. 'Gates of Tomorrow' sits firmly in the latter category, a Gers/Harris/Dickinson collaboration that fails to match any of the previous songs on the record, even the less good ones. Best forgotten, in the author's opinion, but like any Maiden track it is bound to have its own admirers somewhere out there.

'New Frontier'

This is the first writing credit for drummer Nicko McBrain on an Iron Maiden album. With the help of Smith and Dickinson, McBrain (a born-again Christian) expresses his grave concern about human cloning. The track is as forgettable as 'Gates of Tomorrow', and neither song was ever performed live. However, 'New Frontier' is set apart by its gloriously catchy chorus.

'Paschendale'

And now the pendulum swings completely in the opposite direction for a song that can proudly be counted among the best that Iron Maiden ever recorded. Adrian Smith steps out of his comfort zone of shorter and more concise hard rock tracks to attempt his own version of the traditional Maiden epic. The structure of the song is unpredictable and non-formulaic, eschewing the patterns of verses and choruses in favour of a fluid movement through themes and progressions that create a cinematically gripping soundscape full of dark portents.

Steve Harris was inspired by this masterful Smith track to write some of the best lyrics of his career. As the song starts off with what sounds like morse code on McBrain's hi-hat and a quietly lamenting hammer-on-and-pull-off on Smith's guitar, like the sound of children weeping, Harris delivers a shatteringly beautiful war poem for Dickinson to sing: 'In a foreign field he lay / Lonely soldier, unknown grave / On his dying words he prays / Tell the world of Paschendale'. Inspired by the horrors of the Third Battle of Ypres in the First World War, known as the Battle of Paschendaele, the lyrics highlight the meaningless loss of young life that armed conflict entails: 'Rust your bullets with his tears / Let me tell you about his years'. This is truly Smith, Harris, and Maiden on top form, rising through the fire of cannons and machine guns, atmospheric sounds and philharmonic augmentation ably worked into the band's performance fury by producer Kevin Shirley and orchestrator Jeff Bova, to arrive at the end: 'See my spirit on the wind / Across the lines, beyond the hill / Friend and foe will meet again / Those who died at Paschendale'.

The song was the other dramatic cornerstone of the *Dance of Death* live set in 2003–04, next to the title track, and as an introduction Dickinson recited a passage from Wilfred Owen's 1917 poem 'Anthem for Doomed Youth'. The stage was draped in barbed wire and sandbags, with Dickinson dressed in a First World War coat and helmet for a spellbinding performance of intense emotion. 'Paschendale' would also make occasional appearances in the 2010 *The Final Frontier* set but would then be permanently retired.

'Face in the Sand'
The emotional exhaustion that the listener feels after experiencing 'Paschendale' means that the rest of the album has a tough challenge to tackle. Sensibly, the band chooses to place a slow-burner next in the track listing, a Smith/Harris/Dickinson collaboration about the inevitable crumbling of empires. The track is held together by Smith's tasteful guitar playing, and it features the only recorded example of McBrain using double bass drum pedals, which is probably one of the reasons it was never in the frame for live performances.

'Age of Innocence'
Much like 'New Frontier', this song by Murray and Harris is disappointingly unremarkable, except for one thing: a catchy chorus bordering on the poppy.

However, in the aftermath of the previous two song's impactful lyrics, it is a let-down to enter the territory of Harris' occasional preoccupation with reactionary politics. Never performed live, the album would have been none the poorer if this song was dropped.

'JOURNEYMAN'

Thankfully, an inconsistent collection of songs is topped off with a treat. 'Journeyman' is Iron Maiden's first ever all-acoustic recording. Ideally, 'Journeyman' should have followed on directly from 'Paschendale' to round out the album, its uplifting lyrics about the journey of life and creativity bringing an exhausting hour-plus of music to a satisfying conclusion. This song would be a surprising first encore on the 2003–04 *Dance of Death* tour, the guitarists lining up with their acoustics, but it was never subsequently performed again.

RELATED RECORDINGS

The accompanying singles from *Dance of Death* were used to highlight the work of Jeff Bova, the orchestrator that producer Kevin Shirley had hired for both *Dance of Death* and its predecessor *Brave New World*. The 'Wildest Dreams' single featured for the B-sides of its different formats an improvisational session titled 'Pass the Jam', so-called rock mixes (which means without synthesizer orchestration) of 'Blood Brothers' and 'The Nomad' from *Brave New World*, as well as a Bova-heavy orchestral mix of 'Blood Brothers'.

The subsequent 'Rainmaker' single featured an improvised jam titled 'More Tea Vicar' and an orchestral version of 'Dance of Death', as well as 'The Wicker Man' and 'Children of the Damned' live at London's Brixton Academy in March 2002, a part of the Clive Aid initiative to help MS-suffering former drummer Clive Burr.

The 4-song EP 'No More Lies' could just as well be counted as the third single from *Dance of Death*, and it featured the orchestral version of 'Paschendale' and the original electric version (as opposed to the acoustic album version) of 'Journeyman'. Six minutes after the end of 'Journeyman' is hidden a comedy version of 'Age of Innocence' (here subtitled 'How Old?') with drummer Nicko McBrain on hilarious lead vocals.

The *Dance of Death* tour would be thoroughly documented with the *Death on the Road* live album and DVD, both of which are discussed in part four of this book.

LISTENING PREFERENCES

The original release of *Dance of Death* in 2003 was plagued by the decision not to allow Shirley to do a proper mastering of the recording. This was a point of contention between Shirley and Harris that would continue with future albums. However, the 2015 digital remaster of *Dance of Death* sounds much better, and this version is available for streaming and downloads as well as on CD and heavyweight vinyl. Especially the latter, a double LP, makes the album sound the best that it ever did, at least to the author's subjective ears.

14

A Matter of Life and Death

Produced by Kevin Shirley, co-produced by Steve Harris
Released 25 August 2006
Highest chart position and certification at 4/gold (UK), 9/none (US)
Featuring Steve Harris (bass), Dave Murray (guitar), Nicko McBrain (drums), Janick Gers (guitar), Bruce Dickinson (vocals), Adrian Smith (guitar)

Iron Maiden have now transcended aesthetic trends and are liberated from any discussion of musical fashion. *A Matter of Life and Death* is their ultimate and unapologetic statement. It follows in the footsteps of its predecessor, but unlike *Dance of Death* it is completely devoid of filler material. For the first time since the late 1980s, Maiden deliver a record where every single song is thoughtful and interesting enough to warrant its place in the track listing.

By this time, Maiden had embarked on the alternating pattern of new albums and retro tours that would mark their operation for many years to come. In the summer of 2005, they had toured Europe and North America with their *Early Days* set, contextualised by the release of their first history DVD in late 2004, playing material only from their first four studio albums in 1980 to 1983: *Iron Maiden, Killers, The Number of the Beast,* and *Piece of Mind.* After this first so-called history tour, they started writing a new album in late 2005, which was recorded with producer Kevin Shirley in London's Sarm West Studios in early 2006.

After the experiments of the past several album covers, *A Matter of Life and Death* sees Maiden reverting to the cartoon-style artwork of earlier years with an evocative if not quite eye-catching Tim Bradstreet illustration of Eddie and an army of skeletons in the battlefield. It certainly suits the subject matter, packaging as it does a collection of songs very much concerned with the twin topics of war and religion through the ages. Maiden took to the road again in late 2006, performing the album in its entirety (a first and only occurrence in their career) through North America, Japan, and Europe. Another two brief legs followed in March and June of 2007, with a revised setlist lighter on the new material, but Maiden already had their eyes on the 2008 *Powerslave*-centric history tour that would prove a blockbuster.

'Different World'

Although the routine of putting a concise and up-tempo rocker at the head of the album is by now getting tired, 'Different World' is a catchy and uplifting piece of Thin Lizzy-inspired riffs and melodies. Written by Adrian Smith and Steve Harris, and released as the second single from the album in December 2006, the song seems to soften the time-honoured uncompromising Harris perspective to a more mature question of how we see the world from different sides of conflicts and ideologies. As such, it is a very fitting prelude to the darker and more problematic subjects ahead.

'These Colours Don't Run'

The first of several songs written by Adrian Smith, Steve Harris, and Bruce Dickinson in collaboration, 'These Colours Don't Run' thus underlines the high rate of songwriting integration on *A Matter of Life and Death*. Not since the heady days of 1980s masterpieces like *Piece of Mind* and *Seventh Son of a Seventh Son* have Maiden been this cohesive as a unit throughout the writing and recording of an album. A lyric about going off to war and leaving loved ones behind, 'These Colours Don't Run' blends intricate riffs, sudden time changes, patented Maiden gallops, and an inventive middle section of solos and guitar melodies, into a greater whole that indicates a collective surplus of creative ideas.

'Brighter Than a Thousand Suns'

Another Smith/Harris/Dickinson collaboration, this is a song about Robert Oppenheimer and the creation of the atomic bomb during the Second World War. The title is lifted from the controversial 1956 book by Robert Jungk, discussing the making and deployment of the atomic bombs that destroyed Hiroshima and Nagasaki in Japan in 1945. Dickinson's lyrics talk about 'How we made war with the Sun' and 'How we made God with our hands', and Harris' restrained bass playing should be given great credit for providing a thumping groove quite uncharacteristic of Maiden in previous eras.

Many sections of 'Brighter Than a Thousand Suns' are in 7/4 time, something Dickinson had frequent trouble following when the song was performed live. It must be assumed that it was a particularly emotional and surreal experience for band and audience alike when Maiden played this track live in Hiroshima on 26 October 2006, but it was retired permanently at the end of the *A Matter of Life and Death* tour, like most of the album's songs.

'THE PILGRIM'

Next to the opening song, 'The Pilgrim' is the only other concise hard rock track on the album. Written by Janick Gers in collaboration with Harris, it is less remarkable than most other songs on the record, but still a bit of fresh air amid the longer and more complex tracks that dominate this collection, even throwing some Persian scale riffs into the mix.

'THE LONGEST DAY'

Continuing the war epic aesthetic of 'Paschendale' from the previous album, 'The Longest Day' comes impressively close to matching the former. Yet another collaboration between guitarist Smith, bassist Harris, and singer Dickinson, the song takes the listener to the beaches of Normandy in France for Operation Overlord, the Allied D-day landing during the Second World War in 1944. Falling neatly in line with the overarching theme of the album, 'The Longest Day' ratchets up the intensity in terms of dramatic storytelling, speaking of 'the drills to build the machine / To turn men from flesh and blood to steel / From paper soldiers to bodies on the beach / From summer sands to Armageddon's reach'. This track would be an impressive cornerstone of the 2006 live set, including dummy paratroopers falling from the stage ceiling, carrying on the 'Paschendale' war theme of the previous tour.

'OUT OF THE SHADOWS'

That rare thing, an Iron Maiden ballad, which is also another rare thing: a song co-written by Bruce Dickinson and Steve Harris. 'Out of the Shadows' pales in comparison with most other tracks on the record, but it is in itself a pleasant and interesting piece of music, and it also sits rather well as a bit of an intermission between very dramatic tunes either side of it.

'THE REINCARNATION OF BENJAMIN BREEG'

An unconventional choice for first single, released in August 2006, this song is a Dave Murray composition with lyrics and melodies by Steve Harris. Who is Benjamin Breeg? Maiden got some internet attention surrounding this question when the song was released, but it seems that he is merely a fictional character of Harris' imagination. The track builds from a quiet intro into a groovy mid-tempo stomp and a catchy chorus where only the lack of well-judged harmony vocals leaves it somewhat bare and monotonous. Coming on the tail of 'Out of the Shadows', this makes the start of the album's second half a little less impressive than the first. 'The Reincarnation of Benjamin Breeg' was performed throughout the 2006–07 tour and it also reappeared in the 2010 set of *The Final Frontier* tour.

'FOR THE GREATER GOOD OF GOD'
Along with 'The Clansman' on *Virtual XI*, 'Blood Brothers' on *Brave New World*, and the forthcoming 'Hell on Earth' on *Senjutsu*, 'For the Greater Good of God' is one of the best iterations of the patented Steve Harris Celtic-influenced epic composition. Carried across a landscape of high-range melodies by Dickinson on top form, the song is confidently full of ideas for its twists and turns, unlike 'No More Lies' on the previous album, as it debates what love and war means. A cornerstone of the *A Matter of Life and Death* live set in 2006–07, it would make a glorious return in the 'religion' portion of the *Legacy of the Beast* show in 2018–19, finally receiving the live album treatment (albeit with less than impressive sonic results in the muddy mix by Steve Harris and Tony Newton) on *Nights of the Dead, Legacy of the Beast: Live in Mexico City* in 2020.

'LORD OF LIGHT'
If you can get past the chorus melody bearing an uncanny resemblance to the verses in Michael Jackson's 'Give in to Me' from his 1991 *Dangerous* album, 'Lord of Light' is a dark and delightful exercise in heavy metal riffs and vocals of the highest calibre. A Smith and Dickinson concoction, the lyrics seem to discuss Lucifer, the Fallen Archangel, the Morning Star, the Lord of Light, and what this mythical concept could mean in terms of understanding the winding path of humanity through the ages.

'THE LEGACY'
Janick Gers had stepped up to write the impressive title track on *Dance of Death*, and he then turned his contribution of epic material into a tradition with the final song on *A Matter of Life and Death*. 'The Legacy' nearly became the title track too, but the song's lyricist Harris thought it sounded a bit too much like the title of a band's final album. Rounding out an astonishing record in a very suitable manner, 'The Legacy' sums up the subjects of war and faith that have throughout these ten songs been interwoven into multiple abstract and specific essays on the fundamental humanity and will to live that wages battle with destructive forces of death and despair through history. It is certainly not uplifting, the darkness remains with us in this final song, but it is a tale of caution that leaves the ultimate choice in the listener's hands. As such, the song is less of a sure conclusion, both lyrically and musically, and all the better for not being triumphant but pondering. It rounds out Iron Maiden's modern masterpiece.

Related recordings

First single 'The Reincarnation of Benjamin Breeg', released in August 2006, was backed with B-sides recorded live at Maiden's *Radio 1* 'Legends' session in 2006. 'Hallowed Be Thy Name', 'The Trooper' and 'Run to the Hills' were included here, the first two tracks also appearing on the US edition of the 'Different World' single in November, all of them mixed by *Radio 1*'s Jerry Smith.

The European edition of second single 'Different World', meanwhile, was released in several formats in December and included live tracks recorded on the current *A Matter of Life and Death* tour: 'Different World', 'The Reincarnation of Benjamin Breeg', 'Iron Maiden', and 'Fear of the Dark', marking the first Maiden mixes credited to Tony Newton, former Dirty Deeds bassist in the 1990s and ever since then Steve Harris' protégé. To this day, these are the only officially released live recordings from the tour, even though it was reported at the time that Kevin Shirley had mixed a live album.

In addition to the live tracks, the first single was also made available as a promotional edition featuring an edited 'rock club' version of 'The Reincarnation of Benjamin Breeg', while the second single featured a cover version of the 1971 Focus track 'Hocus Pocus'.

Listening preferences

Like *Dance of Death* before it, *A Matter of Life and Death* suffered from poor mastering upon its original release in 2006. Producer Kevin Shirley has stated that he deferred to Steve Harris when the latter elected to ditch a conventional mastering (a process designed to optimize the audio for playback on the common listener's regular sound system) and rather release the recording directly from the studio master, which inevitably means a less than perfect reproduction on private sound systems that do not match the studio sound system. Like the rest of the Maiden catalogue, *A Matter of Life and Death* was remastered for streaming and downloading in 2015, and this version was subsequently released on CD and heavyweight vinyl, where the latter seems to be the fullest and most pleasant representation to date.

15

The Final Frontier

Produced by Kevin Shirley, co-produced by Steve Harris
Released 13 August 2010
Highest chart position and certification at 1/gold (UK), 4/none (US)
Featuring Steve Harris (bass), Dave Murray (guitar), Nicko McBrain (drums), Janick Gers (guitar), Bruce Dickinson (vocals), Adrian Smith (guitar)

Iron Maiden had now become one of the biggest heavy metal bands on the planet once again, largely thanks to the huge success of their 2008–09 *Somewhere Back in Time World Tour*. Featuring a modernised version of the *Powerslave* stage set from 1984–85 and focusing exclusively on their 1980s material (with the exception of 1992's 'Fear of the Dark', which would from now on be omnipresent), this second so-called history tour had brought massive media attention because of the Ed Force One airplane that singer Bruce Dickinson flew the band around the world in, as well as the trip down memory lane with a setlist that fans could barely have dreamed of ten years earlier. Dickinson has stated that the tour's success was a double-edged sword in that it made it tough for Maiden to do a new album, arguably making them overthink the importance of following up not just the tour, but also the brilliant *A Matter of Life and Death* from 2006.

In an apparent attempt to recapture the vibe of the 1980s, or perhaps because bassist Steve Harris was now residing in the Bahamas, Maiden chose to record their new album at Compass Point Studios in Nassau, the site of recordings for *Piece of Mind* (1983), *Powerslave* (1984) and *Somewhere in Time* (1986). After writing sessions in Paris, France in late 2009, Maiden and their regular producer Kevin Shirley recorded basic tracks for the new material in Nassau in early 2010. Truth be told, as Dickinson relates in his autobiography, the state of Compass Point was poor, and Shirley ended up bringing in almost all the equipment needed for the sessions. The producer would subsequently conduct overdubs of vocals, guitars, and synthesizers, as well as the mix, in his own studio The Cave in Malibu, California. This might go some way to explain how *The Final Frontier* became arguably the best-sounding of all Iron Maiden albums in the period from 2000. It seems that Shirley focused on getting the best possible drum sound from Nicko McBrain in Nassau, along with Harris' bass and the rhythms, riffs and chords of guitarists Dave Murray, Adrian Smith, and Janick Gers. The producer's firm control of the overdubs and the mix, and this time also a properly sophisticated mastering process, yielded a warm and strong band sound.

Maiden would pattern their next tour on the 2003 *Dance of Death* campaign, launching the trek ahead of the album's release and including only first single 'El Dorado' in the set in the summer of 2010. But in reaction to the 2008–09 history tour, the 2010 summer tour would focus heavily and refreshingly on the band's post-2000 output. When the 2011 portion of the tour rolled out, once again aboard Ed Force One, there were more new songs in the set while the classics reverted to a very predictable collection of tracks like 'The Trooper' and 'The Number of the Beast'. After the powerful demonstrations of the 2008–09 retro set and the 2010 modern set, the 2011 tour was the point where fans and critics alike started to think that perhaps Maiden had now spent what they had in terms of invention and adventure. This would turn out to be not quite true, although the subsequent *Maiden England* history tour in 2012–14 was less celebrated than its 2008–09 *Somewhere Back in Time* predecessor. A major bump in the road, in the form of Dickinson's life-threatening cancer diagnosis, would have to be overcome before Maiden once again returned to their full glory.

The album artwork was once again created by the intestines-fixated Melvyn Grant, who had previously done *Fear of the Dark* and *Virtual XI* in the 1990s, this time contriving a space creature Eddie that bears very little resemblance to any earlier incarnation. Meanwhile, *The Final Frontier* continued Iron Maiden's momentum in the new millennium. It saw them receiving plenty of critical accolades and even a Grammy Award for 'El Dorado', but this era also marked the dawn of a paradox in Maiden's commercial reputation: As the sales of physical CD albums plunged worldwide, Maiden's dependable ability to sell considerable amounts early in an album's run (fans do buy it, after all) would take them to the top of charts around the globe for the first time since their 1980s heyday, even if they sold nowhere near the amounts of records that they shifted back then. Simply put, when everybody sells less, there are not as many sales needed to reach the top of the charts.

'Satellite 15 ... The Final Frontier'

Bruce Dickinson had thought of the album title a long time before Maiden recorded the music for it, mischievously thinking that *The Final Frontier* might spark discussions about whether this was in fact to be their last album, their fifteenth. However, the song of the same title was written by Adrian Smith and Steve Harris, discussing the emotions of being stranded in space with no chance of returning to Earth, facing a final frontier of both space and death.

The mysterious and frequently atonal 'Satellite 15' intro piece is a refreshing start after a string of albums that all started with an up-tempo hard rock song. The downside is the decision to use Smith's demo recording as a bed instead of re-recording it properly, the sound being sub-par and even some glitches in the drum programming sticking out. 'The Final Frontier' itself is a less remarkable mid-tempo rocker, which is still a pleasant listen due to the very enjoyable soundscape that Shirley and the band achieve. This latter half of the track was released as a music video in July 2010 and the whole of 'Satellite 15 ... The Final Frontier' would be the opening number on the 2011 *The Final Frontier* tour.

'El Dorado'

The first taster from the album, released as a digital single in June 2010, 'El Dorado' is another Smith and Harris track that also includes lyrics and melodies from Dickinson. It is a groovy and riff-laden mid-tempo affair with a soaring chorus that exploits the very highest reaches of the singer's range. The lyrics are obviously inspired by the global financial crisis of 2007–08, told from the point of view of 'a clever banker's face, with just a letter out of place.' 'El Dorado' is the first of the album's three stand-out tracks, Shirley's muscular production being essential to its weight and force, and it would be performed on both the 2010 and 2011 portions of Maiden's *The Final Frontier* world tour.

'Mother of Mercy'

Another mid-tempo riff-fest, even slower than the previous song, 'Mother of Mercy' was written by Smith and Harris, but it leaves no lasting impression and was never performed live. In truth, this is one of the two or three tracks that could have been cut to bring the album's running time down from its needlessly excessive 76 minutes to something closer to one hour. Still, it never really gets boring to listen to Smith's guitar work.

'Coming Home'

The second of the album's three stand-out tracks, 'Coming Home' is Iron Maiden's version of the generic power ballad of ages past. Another Smith/Harris/Dickinson collaboration, the lyrical point of view is that of Dickinson looking out from his airplane on to the Earth below and reflecting on traveling and touring: 'As the waves and echoes of the towns become the ghosts of time.' There is a palpable emotion of returning to his homeland and the sense that all of Earth is so small in the scheme of things: 'Stretch the fingers of my hand / Cover countries with my span / Just a lonely satellite / A speck of dust in cosmic sand.'

This is a truly inspired piece of Maiden music, and unlike any other track they have recorded. It was a cornerstone of the set on the 2011 *The Final Frontier* tour and issued as a radio promo track in October 2010. 'Coming Home' is a song that fires up the same sort of bonding emotions as 'Blood Brothers' on *Brave New World*, creating that field of dissolving tensions where the audience feels a connection not only with the band but with each other, and yet Maiden have surprisingly never revisited this track on any later tour.

'THE ALCHEMIST'

The shortest track on the album, this up-tempo rocker by Janick Gers in collaboration with Harris and Dickinson is enjoyable and yet quite unremarkable in the context of the previous tracks 'El Dorado' and 'Coming Home'. Playing it too safe might be its problem, although the chorus is satisfyingly melodic with a blanket of harmony guitars underpinning Dickinson's delicate vocal delivery.

'ISLE OF AVALON'

Here begins a second half of *The Final Frontier* where no less than five tracks compete for the spot of the album's conventional 'epic'. This is a major pacing mistake, as the songs get in each other's way and the listener is soon too exhausted to give them all their fair shake. But none of them, in retrospect, gets close to matching the power of the previous couple of albums' major works like 'Paschendale' and 'For the Greater Good of God'. Sensibly, Maiden only performed two of these tracks on tour, and 'Isle of Avalon' was not among them. Written by Smith and Harris, the song is meandering and directionless, particularly in its jam-oriented and semi-improvised middle section in 7/4 time. Some fans will find things to enjoy here, but in the author's opinion the song is woefully undercooked.

'STARBLIND'

'Starblind', a Smith/Harris/Dickinson composition, starts off more promising than the previous track, but after a rather monotonous run of verses and choruses it fails to take flight, losing its way with yet another middle section in 7/4 time, as though Maiden are very impressed with having discovered a new time signature. It was never performed live.

'The Talisman'

In contrast, here is a track with purpose and structure that would also go down well live on stage. The third of the album's three stand-out tracks, 'The Talisman' is another proud addition to the Gers repertoire of later career epics, with lyrics and melodies by Harris. A hymn to the ocean and the migration from troubles into new worlds and lives, the song features massively impressive performances from both Dickinson and McBrain. It would be a cornerstone of the 2011 setlist, but it was then retired permanently.

'The Man Who Would Be King'

As soon as 'The Talisman' has regained momentum for *The Final Frontier*, it is lost again with the lone Dave Murray composition on the album. Written in collaboration with Harris, 'The Man Who Would Be King' is yawn-inducingly pedestrian and directionless, and like 'Mother of Mercy' it is a tune that should have been dropped to save the album from a needlessly lengthy running time with too many overlong songs. It was never performed live by Iron Maiden.

'When the Wild Wind Blows'

The record buckles under the weight of these unrealised epics, making it hard for the final track to get a fair appraisal. 'When the Wild Wind Blows' is the only song on the album written by Harris alone, and it is a fittingly ambivalent conclusion to an album of some major highlights and too many disappointing entries. Harris' dramatic lyrics of a nuclear holocaust misunderstanding are very moving, and as always, they are delivered with faultless empathy and conviction by Dickinson. However, by now these Celtic-inspired melodies and the Em—C—G—D chord progression is all too familiar to arouse engagement, Harris' modern aesthetic arguably having outstayed its welcome by a considerable margin. Despite its charms, the song could conceivably have been shortened by almost half its running time without losing any essential elements.

Certainly, Maiden had placed the bar higher than expected with their post-2000 run of albums, particularly the filler-less *A Matter of Life and Death*, but the band seemed to have arrived at a point of anaemia that would also permeate the stage production and setlist for the 2011 *The Final Frontier* tour. The drop in surplus energy and quality songwriting from the previous album is similar to the lapse from the career high of *Seventh Son of a Seventh Son* in 1988 to the under-cooked *No Prayer for the Dying* in 1990. Thankfully, *The Final Frontier* would not be what many feared at the time: the final Iron Maiden album.

RELATED RECORDINGS

The Final Frontier marked the point in time when Iron Maiden all but stopped releasing physical editions of singles, and so was lost the age of the B-sides. The major related recording is the live album and concert video *En Vivo!*, recorded and filmed in Santiago, Chile on the 2011 tour and discussed briefly in part four of this book.

LISTENING PREFERENCES

As previously noted, it could be argued that *The Final Frontier* features the best production work that Kevin Shirley ever did for Iron Maiden. The fine recordings and mix were further enhanced by the mastering process that was overseen by the legendary Bob Ludwig at Gateway Mastering. Ludwig made his name at Sterling Sound in the 1970s and is one of the superstar names of mastering for very good reasons. Thus, the original CD release of *The Final Frontier* from 2010 is still a good listen, while the 2015 digital remaster that is currently also available on CD and vinyl comes a very close second. Like *Brave New World* before it, this is a later era Maiden album where you can't really go wrong either way you listen.

The Book of Souls

Produced by Kevin Shirley, co-produced by Steve Harris
Released 4 September 2015
Highest chart position and certification at 1/gold (UK), 4/none (US)
Featuring Steve Harris (bass), Dave Murray (guitar), Nicko McBrain (drums), Janick Gers (guitar), Bruce Dickinson (vocals), Adrian Smith (guitar)

After the conclusion of Iron Maiden's third so-called history tour, the *Seventh Son*-centric *Maiden England* tour in 2012–14, the band set up camp at Studio Guillaume Tell in Paris, France for writing and recording sessions in late 2014. Using the same studio as they had done for *Brave New World* fifteen years earlier reportedly created very good vibes, but at the end of the sessions singer Bruce Dickinson was worried about a lump on his neck. Doctors soon confirmed the shock news: neck and throat cancer. In January and February 2015, Dickinson underwent radiation therapy to remove tumours in his neck and tongue, and manager Rod Smallwood only released the news to the public once the treatment was completed and the prognosis for a successful recovery was good.

Iron Maiden's plans were slightly delayed, touring being pushed from 2015 into 2016, and *The Book of Souls* was released in the late summer of 2015. This is Iron Maiden's longest studio album ever, clocking in at a monstrous 92 minutes, and it was released as a double CD and triple LP in addition to digital versions. Artist Mark Wilkinson was called in to create a recognisable Eddie, this time as a tribal Mayan warrior with a taste for cutting out hearts, and the accompanying *The Book of Souls* world tour in 2016–17 was the most inspired stage production Maiden had taken on the road since the *Powerslave*-recreation on the *Somewhere Back in Time* tour in 2008–09. In fact, the band seemed reborn with Dickinson's return from the edge of cancer's abyss, revelling in their new material and revisiting rare songs like 'Children of the Damned' and 'Powerslave'. The album charted high in many countries, although sales were low compared with the 1980s, and the band took to the skies for yet another Dickinson-managed Ed Force One adventure around the globe.

'If Eternity Should Fail'
Originally written for Bruce Dickinson's next solo album, which eventually arrived as *The Mandrake Project* in 2024, he gave it up for Iron Maiden when Steve Harris suggested it would make a good opening song on *The Book of Souls*. Although Dickinson's solo partner Roy Z (composer, guitarist, producer) is nowhere to be found in the credits, it is frankly very hard to believe that he had nothing to do with this track. 'If Eternity Should Fail' is easily the moodiest and most atmospheric opening to a Maiden record since 'Sign of the Cross' on *The X Factor* in 1995, and it sets the tone very properly with its lyrics announcing that 'Here is the soul of a man'. The track would also open the show in dramatic fashion on the 2016–17 *The Book of Souls* world tour.

'Speed of Light'
The first of a fair number of shortish up-tempo rock tunes on the album, 'Speed of Light' is a science fiction romp written by Adrian Smith in collaboration with Dickinson. It is not a remarkable song, but the energy of the band lifts it into the realm of entertaining, and it is topped off with masterful hard rock guitar solos from both Smith and Dave Murray. 'Speed of Light' was released as a single from the album in August 2015, and it was performed on tour in 2016–17.

'The Great Unknown'
The first entry on the album credited to Smith in collaboration with Harris, 'The Great Unknown' takes a while to get going. But it does sport one of the catchiest and most melodic choruses on the record, one that is for once not repeated too many times. 'The Great Unknown' was not included on the 2016 portion of the tour, but rather surprisingly replaced 'Hallowed Be Thy Name' on the 2017 legs that encompassed Europe and North America.

'The Red and the Black'
Harris' songs had steadily gotten longer and longer over the years, and at last he arrived at a point just nine seconds short of the running-time record held by 1984's 'Rime of the Ancient Mariner'. Unfortunately, 'The Red and

the Black' is no match for its predecessor. Pleasantly engaging in its first half, apart from the embarrassing acoustic bass intro that blatantly rips off some of Howard Shore's *The Lord of the Rings* film score, it loses its way around the mid-point and only comes back into focus at the very end of its nearly 14 minutes. Credit must be given, however, to Nicko McBrain for keeping a solid groove throughout the meandering song, and to Dickinson for delivering the labyrinthine lyrics with customary conviction. Much of the track is given over to either guitar melodies or wordless chants that were practically designed for audience singalongs, so 'The Red and the Black' became a cornerstone of the 2016–17 *The Book of Souls* setlist.

'When the River Runs Deep'

Never performed live, 'When the River Runs Deep' is another fairly short song co-written by Smith and Harris. With Smith's much-publicised passion for fishing, one could be forgiven for suspecting his mind and hand behind lyrics like 'When the river runs deep and the line breaks', but this is in fact yet another bleak and world-weary piece of Harris' mind. Although the chorus is melodically appealing, the song must be considered filler material. This is also one of several instances on the album where the listener experiences a disconcerting bit of *déjà vu*, with the main riff strongly reminiscent of the riff in 'Man on the Edge' on 1995's *The X Factor*.

'The Book of Souls'

Janick Gers had originally presented this groovy and complex idea to Harris when the band were working on their previous album *The Final Frontier*. At the time, Harris felt they had enough good material and suggested to Gers that they could keep this one for a later opportunity. Harris' admittedly inelegant lyrics, where the album's title was found, discuss the rise and fall of the Mesoamerican Maya civilisation in Central America. However, the most remarkable aspect of the song is the fact that Gers here delivers a stand-out epic track for the fourth album in a row, cementing his importance to the modern Iron Maiden oeuvre. 'The Book of Souls' was a cornerstone on the 2016–17 tour and particularly goosebump-inducing on the nights when Dickinson nailed his very demanding vocal performance.

'Death or Glory'

A throwback to the dogfights in the sky of both 1984's 'Aces High' and 1990's 'Tailgunner', this song by Smith and Dickinson is a weirdly quick-paced shuffle that would become an audience favourite on the tour due to Dickinson's manic insistence on getting the crowds to 'climb like a monkey' with their hand gestures. Fun for some, annoying for others, the track is nevertheless unremarkable in comparison with the best the album has to offer.

'Shadows of the Valley'

The second song on the album never to be performed in concert, 'Shadows of the Valley' is another case of *déjà vu* where co-writer Gers nearly imitates the opening guitar figure from the *Somewhere in Time* classic 'Wasted Years' while Harris' words even namecheck the same album's 'Sea of Madness'. The lyrics depict a dark and disturbing scene of fantasy and horror, lamenting that 'without sunlight things are born to the dead of nightmares' and facing 'a walk in the shadow of the valley of death, knowing I'll take my last breath'. As usual with Harris, dark images are easily conjured even if the precise meaning of the words might elude us, but the shuffle-beat music on this track is directionless and forgettable.

'Tears of a Clown'

Movingly inspired by the tragic passing of actor and comedian Robin Williams in 2014, 'Tears of a Clown' is a mid-tempo track by Smith and Harris that in ages gone by could conceivably have been a single release. Dickinson's emotional performance is essential to the successful lift of this rather simplistic track. It was featured in the 2016 setlist but replaced by golden oldie 'Wrathchild' for the 2017 legs of Maiden's *The Book of Souls* tour.

'The Man of Sorrows'

Not related to the 1997 Dickinson solo track 'Man of Sorrows' on his *Accident of Birth* album, this is the third track on the album never performed on stage. The term is biblical and describes the state and suffering of Jesus Christ at the end of his life on Earth, in visual arts denoting the depiction of Christ with his wounds from the crucifixion. This song is Murray's only writing credit on the record, in collaboration with Harris, and it is unfortunately akin to his track 'The Man Who Would Be King' on the previous album *The Final Frontier* in that it is utterly forgettable. By this point of the album, it is clear that at least three songs could have been removed to tighten the running time and improve the listening experience.

'Empire of the Clouds'

Just when you thought the Harris record could never be beaten, Dickinson concocts a song that usurps 'Rime of the Ancient Mariner' as the longest Maiden track ever. At 18 minutes long, 'Empire of the Clouds' is a complex and sprawling composition that the singer worked out on a grand piano over the course of the 2014 Paris sessions. Lyrically inspired by the catastrophic crash of the British airship R101 in 1930, Dickinson's dramatic music is aided by the patient contributions of the band and the synthesizer orchestrations of Jeff Bova, who had previously worked with them on *Brave New World* and

Dance of Death. If ever Iron Maiden were to stage a collaboration with a symphony orchestra, this work must surely be on the list.

The delicate piano and cello melodies in the early parts of the song are arguably the most moving and elegant features of the entire composition, the subsequent grander and more dramatic parts involving the full-on band treatment sounding a little contrived by comparison. The song would surprisingly and uncompromisingly be issued as the second single from the album in April 2016, albeit only as a 12-inch vinyl picture disc for the annual event called Record Store Day. 'Empire of the Clouds' is the fourth and final song on *The Book of Souls* never to be performed in concert.

Related recordings

The age of physical single releases with more or less interesting B-side material was now definitively over. The picture disc release of 'Empire of the Clouds' carried for its B-side a 21-minute narration from Dickinson and McBrain about the making of the song. Other than this, the major related recording is the 2017 live album *The Book of Souls: Live Chapter*, which is discussed briefly in part four of this book.

Listening preferences

The mastering of *The Book of Souls* was handled by Ade Emsley at Table of Tone Mastering, who would at this point also co-head the 2015 remastering of the Maiden back catalogue with Tony Newton. Whether the mix or the mastering is the problem, the album sounds less punchy and warm than its predecessor *The Final Frontier*. It should be noted, however, that the heavyweight vinyl edition of *The Book of Souls* sounds better than the CD or the streaming and download version, at least to the author's subjective ears, and this might be credited to the additional vinyl mastering by Chris Bellman at Bernie Grundman.

17

Senjutsu

Produced by Kevin Shirley, co-produced by Steve Harris
Released 3 September 2021
Highest chart position and certification at 2/gold (UK), 3/none (US)
Featuring Steve Harris (bass), Dave Murray (guitar), Nicko McBrain (drums), Janick Gers (guitar), Bruce Dickinson (vocals), Adrian Smith (guitar)

After the successful recovery of singer Bruce Dickinson from neck and throat cancer, and the massive *The Book of Souls* world tour in 2016 to 2017, Iron Maiden cycled back into history mode and launched their *Legacy of the Beast* world tour in 2018. Inspired by the Maiden video game of the same name, the stage production would move through three different worlds or themes, or levels if you like: war, religion, and hell. The setlist focused largely on the band's classic 1980s period, even resurrecting the long lost 'Flight of Icarus', but also covered later eras with tracks like 'Sign of the Cross' and 'The Clansman' from the 1990s, and 'The Wicker Man' and 'For the Greater Good of God' from the 2000s.

In a novel approach to creating new music, Maiden decided to write and record at Studio Guillaume Tell in Paris, during spring of 2019, in a break between legs of the tour. The original plan was to wrap up the *Legacy of the Beast* tour in the summer of 2020 and immediately release the new album after the end of the tour. However, the coronavirus pandemic intervened, and Maiden's touring was put on hold through 2020 and 2021. It was eventually decided to release the new album, titled *Senjutsu*, in September 2021, and subsequently to work some of the new songs into the setlist for the last portion of the *Legacy of the Beast* tour that eventually rolled out in the summer of 2022.

As if realising that *Senjutsu* could very well be the last ever Iron Maiden album, bassist Steve Harris put more of his own ideas into the recording than he had done since the 1990s, the result of which was no less than four epic Harris compositions with three of them rounding out the album with running times of over 10 minutes each. Mixed with this were numerous entries credited to Dickinson and to guitarists Adrian Smith and Janick Gers. Once again produced by Kevin Shirley, the album sounds very much akin to its predecessor *The Book of Souls* from 2015, and clocks in at a total of almost 82 minutes, making it the second longest Maiden studio album.

Due to the re-structuring of touring plans that was made necessary by the two-year touring gap during the pandemic, *Senjutsu* would be the first Iron Maiden studio album with no accompanying album tour. The record's first three tracks, and a stage dressing inspired by the samurai aesthetic of Mark Wilkinson's album artwork, were added to the opening of the set on the 2022 *Legacy of the Beast* tour, while the 2023–24 *The Future Past* tour would see *Senjutsu* material combined with a focus on the classic *Somewhere in Time* album from 1986, much to the delight of fans who had always thought the latter under-employed in Maiden's setlists over the decades. *Senjutsu* would become one of Iron Maiden's highest-charting albums of all time, but it would ultimately sell less than any Maiden album since *Virtual XI* in 1998.

'Senjutsu'

After the previous two albums' more adventurous opening numbers, Iron Maiden continue in the same vein with 'Senjutsu', a muscular composition by Adrian Smith and Steve Harris that bulges and swings in something best described as a heavy metal waltz beat. Nicko McBrain's drumming and drum sound deserves special praise for the way the track ebbs and flows through its considerable running time of more than 8 minutes, slowly telling the tale of warriors committed to protecting a great defensive wall.

Iron Maiden's press release claimed that *Senjutsu* is a term for strategy and tactics as applied to warfare, but this seems rather to indicate the ancient book *The Art of War* by military strategist and philosopher Sun Tzu. *Senjutsu* is in fact a term for a specialised field of *jutsu* (the mystical ninja martial arts) that involves the exploitation of natural energies in a practitioner's own body as well as their surroundings. Additionally, Bruce Dickinson has stated several times that Harris is unconcerned with syntax and intelligibility when writing lyrics, giving the melody precedence over any other factor, and this certainly leads to song lyrics that on the printed page seem unintelligible and sometimes suffer plain incorrect English. 'Senjutsu' is the first of many examples on the album, but this does not hinder Dickinson from elevating the song to a performance of supreme drama. The track was the opening number for the 2022 *Legacy of the Beast* tour, but it was then retired from the setlist.

'STRATEGO'
Written by Janick Gers in conjunction with Harris, 'Stratego' is another weird song title, literally being the name of a strategy board game. The song itself, however, is a pleasant piece of melodic hard rock in the time-honoured Iron Maiden gallop. It nearly overflows with beautiful vocal and guitar harmonies, although the Shirley mix seems to settle a little more solidly on the next couple of tracks. 'Stratego' was issued as a video and digital single ahead of the album's release, in August 2021, and it was performed on the 2022 tour before being dropped from the set.

'THE WRITING ON THE WALL'
The album's first video and digital single, released in July 2021, 'The Writing on the Wall' is a mid-paced classic rock number by Smith in conjunction with Dickinson. Decrying humanity's innate fear of change and reluctance to learn from history, the lyrics spell out the doom of humankind in their inability to adapt their minds and hearts: 'A tide of change is coming and that is what you fear / The earthquake is a-coming, but you don't want to hear.' The writing is on the wall for the people of Earth in the face of the climate breakdown and any number of political and ideological situations around the globe, and maybe this is part of the explanation for the song's success on stage. It was predictably included in the 2022 rounding-off of the *Legacy of the Beast* tour, but it was then more surprisingly very well received as part of the *Future Past* set in 2023 alongside *Somewhere in Time* classics.

'LOST IN A LOST WORLD'
The first of the album's four solo compositions by Harris, 'Lost in a Lost World' clocks in just shy of 10 minutes and has never been performed live. The opening section's acoustic guitars and vocals, as well as the ending's delicate combo of vocals and a lead guitar melody, are the best features of a track that gets more anonymous during its stomping middle section. In particular, it must be noted that guitarist Dave Murray has a sophisticated ability to play melody along with Dickinson's singing. Harris' lyrics seem to lament the tragic fate of North American indigenous peoples and to place hope in the promise of an afterlife: 'As the clouds all drift away now / Until we meet again.'

'DAYS OF FUTURE PAST'
The album's shortest song at 4 minutes, 'Days of Future Past' is a riffy hard rocker from Smith and Dickinson. It is arguably one of the least remarkable songs on the record, along with 'Stratego' and the upcoming 'The Time Machine', but the fact that it is still very enjoyable proves that *Senjutsu* is a

considerably stronger album than both its predecessors, *The Book of Souls* and *The Final Frontier*. 'Days of Future Past' would have been a strange omission from the 2023 *The Future Past* tour, and it took its place as one of the early *Senjutsu* songs in the set that followed the one-two *Somewhere in Time* opening of 'Caught Somewhere in Time' and 'Stranger in a Strange Land'.

'The Time Machine'
'The Time Machine' was also a thematically appropriate track in the 2023 setlist, but it is in truth a less remarkable song from Gers and Harris, lacking a powerful chorus. What ensures that it works for a Maiden audience is the middle section's flurry of singable guitar melodies.

'Darkest Hour'
A rare Iron Maiden ballad, in the tradition of 'Out of the Shadows' on *A Matter of Life and Death*, this Smith and Dickinson composition takes as its lyrical subject the significance of Winston Churchill to the fortunes of Great Britain in the Second World War, focusing on the dark depression of the nation, and its protagonist, following the Dunkirk evacuation in 1940. It has not been performed live, but it is another showcase for Dickinson's storytelling abilities and world-class hard rock singing, even as he eases into his sixties.

'Death of the Celts'
The first of the Harris *Senjutsu* epics to be performed live on the 2023 *The Future Past* tour, up against 1986's 'Alexander the Great' in the middle of the set, 'Death of the Celts' is for all intents and purposes a sequel to 'The Clansman' on the 1998 *Virtual XI* album. Not quite as strong, not quite as catchy, but the guitar interplay between Murray, Smith and Gers ensures that there is enough interesting playing for the listener to lose oneself in.

'The Parchment'
Another Harris entry, this track is reminiscent of the mood and sound of the classic 1983 *Piece of Mind* album, the influence of Eastern scales recalling that record's 'To Tame a Land' and providing a welcome respite from the Celtic aesthetic that dominates Harris' post-1995 compositions. 'The Parchment' was never performed live, but it builds slowly and delicately through fine weaving of guitars and another strong vocal performance. The lyrics fall in line with most other Harris lyrics on the album in its darkness and despair, ending on a note of wanting to escape: 'Like a fire in the sky / I can feel strength return / Heading for afterlife / Meet me there'.

'Hell on Earth'
At this point the listener might start to worry about Harris' mental health. All the lyrics for his solo compositions on *Senjutsu* are dark and pessimistic, bordering on morbid. 'Hell on Earth' follows 'Lost in a Lost World', 'Death of the Celts' and 'The Parchment' with equally bleak observations about the misery of life and the liberation of death. The lyrics of the chorus go 'And when I leave this world / I hope to see you all again / On the other side of this hell on earth', and the lasting impression is that of a very tired soul.

Of course, there is a danger of reading too much into it. But with such a mass of lyrics all going in the same direction? Depending on one's point of view, this could all be very disturbing, or on the other hand: Here is an empathetic reaching out to troubled people around the world and a sense of sharing the burden. Whatever the writer's emotional intent, the music of 'Hell on Earth' is among some of Harris' later career best, particularly the beautiful and uplifting melodies of the chorus, which rather strangely is performed only once during a running time of more than 11 minutes. The song worked surprisingly well as the first encore in the *Future Past* setlist in 2023 and 2024, and it would not disgrace itself if it truly was to be Iron Maiden's swansong.

The 2024 leg of the *Future Past* tour turned out to be the swansong for Nicko McBrain, who retired from touring with Maiden after the final show in Sao Paulo, Brazil. After forty-two years as the inimitable Maiden drummer, McBrain stepped down gracefully and handed the drumsticks over to Simon Dawson, Steve Harris' rhythm section partner in British Lion. The fiftieth anniversary *Run for Your Lives* tour that kicked off in 2025 will continue into 2026, but whether Iron Maiden will ever make another record remains to be seen.

Related recordings
The singles 'The Writing on the Wall' and 'Stratego' were only released as videos and digital tracks, and there are no other recordings related to *Senjutsu* unless Maiden use recordings from the *Future Past* tour for a live album or concert video as their career inevitably begins to fade into its twilight years.

Listening preferences
Like its predecessor *The Book of Souls*, *Senjutsu* was mastered by Ade Emsley at Table of Tone Mastering. This time the listening experience is more comfortable, with better definition for the guitar mix and a slightly more precise representation of the drums. The album sounds equal in its CD and heavyweight vinyl editions, and it is also pleasantly well-rounded when streamed from a high-quality service through high-quality speakers or headphones.

PART FOUR
Other Recordings

18

Live Albums

From the very start of their career, Iron Maiden was always known as first and foremost a live band, a group that saw the stage and the interaction with an audience as the chief reason for their existence. For band leader Steve Harris in particular, recreating the energy and aesthetics of Maiden's live performances in the studio would be a perpetual challenge. Despite this, Iron Maiden did not actually release a live album until after their fifth studio album *Powerslave* (1984). There were occasional live B-sides and EPs earlier, all of them previously discussed while outlining Maiden's studio albums in the book's part one, but Maiden's first and only live record in the 1980s was *Live After Death* (1985). There would be several more in the 1990s, except for the Blaze Bayley period, and after 2000 the Maiden live albums would become as regular as their studio records.

LIVE AFTER DEATH
Producer Martin Birch recorded Iron Maiden's *Powerslave* show over four nights at Hammersmith Odeon in London, England in October 1984 and another four nights at Long Beach Arena in California, USA in March 1985. Released on 14 October 1985, the first three vinyl sides of *Live After Death* were taken from Long Beach, as was the accompanying video release, while the final vinyl side added tracks recorded at Hammersmith. Birch mixed the recordings in July and August 1985, a process that also included re-recording parts of Bruce Dickinson's lead vocals and Adrian Smith's guitars and backing vocals.

Live After Death has gone down in history as one of the greatest live albums ever made. It is certainly the yardstick against which all subsequent Iron Maiden live records are measured. Focusing heavily on the three most recent Maiden albums (*The Number of the Beast*, *Piece of Mind* and *Powerslave*), the record documents Maiden at the height of their original golden age and the zenith of their 1980s popularity in the United States. While it is obvious that Dickinson has started to lose some of his effortless range due to the exhaustion of Maiden's relentless touring, making it easy to note where the studio overdubs are patched in during tracks like 'The Trooper' and 'Hallowed Be Thy Name', a great highlight of the album is the masterclass in heavy metal guitar playing provided by Smith and his partner Dave Murray. Prime examples of this are the twin centrepieces of the *World Slavery Tour* setlist, 'Rime of the Ancient Mariner' and 'Powerslave', delivered with atmospheric gusto and dramatic aplomb in a way that only classic era Iron Maiden could do. The technical ability of this Maiden line-up, underpinned by faultless efforts from Steve Harris and Nicko McBrain, combines well with the finely tuned emotion of their performances.

There are some obscure recordings related to *Live After Death*. Maiden released two singles to accompany the album in 1985, 'Running Free (live)' and 'Run to the Hills (live)'. The former featured as its B-side 'Sanctuary (live)' from the Long Beach concerts and the rare 'Murders in the Rue Morgue (live)' from the Hammersmith recordings. The latter single featured 'Phantom of the Opera (live)' from the Hammersmith vinyl side of the album and the extremely rare 'Losfer Words (Big 'Orra) (live)' from Hammersmith prior to being dropped for good later in the tour. Derek Riggs created a memorable illustration for the 'Run to the Hills (live)' single where Eddie plays the Phantom of the Gaston Leroux-inspired story against an atmospheric backdrop of, you guessed it, hills. For the fan and collector, these singles complete the *World Slavery Tour* showcase that is so vividly presented by the album and the concert video.

The setlist of the 1985 American leg of the tour opened with the double whammy of 'Aces High' and '2 Minutes to Midnight' from *Powerslave*, before showcasing *Piece of Mind* nicely with the triple treat of 'The Trooper', 'Revelations' and 'Flight of Icarus'. A great plus with *Live After Death* is the fourth vinyl side that features rarer tracks from the European leg of the tour, including 'Children of the Damned' and 'Die with Your Boots On'. It makes for an extended and comprehensive package that highlights Maiden's incredible opening salvo of five great studio albums in as many years. Not a single song could easily have been dropped from this record, and yet there are many that could have been added. *Live After Death* endures as the essential Iron Maiden live album, as important to their legacy as *Made in Japan* is to Deep Purple or *KISS Alive!* to KISS.

A Real Live One

1993 was a strange year for Maiden fans. As the band was about to launch several highly anticipated live albums for the first time since the colossal

Live After Death almost eight years earlier, Dickinson announced his departure from the band. When *A Real Live One* arrived on 22 March, the grief of the singer's imminent departure was for many fans coupled with disappointment in Harris' debut as sole Iron Maiden producer. Without Martin Birch, Harris seemed determined to deliver a low-fi experience: dry and reverb-less guitars and vocals, over painfully thin-sounding drums.

For some reason, Maiden and management decided against doing a double live album that presented their *Fear of the Dark* set in its entirety, opting to fill *A Real Live One* with tracks from their four albums in the post-*Live After Death* period from 1986 to 1992, while setting aside the 1980 to 1984 tracks for the subsequent *A Real Dead One*. The tracks are also recorded in many different cities throughout the 1992 European tour, which serves to showcase more fans but unfortunately denies the listener a proper concert vibe.

'Fear of the Dark (live)' was the single off the album, and this might have been the point at which the track turned into an omnipresent song in Maiden setlists thanks to the audience participation that Harris decided to bring up in the mix. Whatever your own opinion of *A Real Live One*, this is a very different proposition to *Live After Death*. It is certainly performed with fire and passion, both Dickinson and McBrain sounding on top form throughout, even if the primitive production values highlight every bad guitar note along the way and stubbornly refuses to facilitate the listening experience.

A REAL DEAD ONE

Quite how this idea for an album title managed to survive the friction-filled 1993 tour with the soon-to-be-gone Dickinson, as well as the uncertain prospects of Maiden with a new singer in a music world increasingly hostile to their brand of metal, is anybody's guess. It would be hard to come up with a worse contender for album title even if Dickinson had stayed in the band. *A Real Dead One* is the counterpart to *A Real Live One*, featuring the pre-1985 tracks in Maiden's *Fear of the Dark* set (slightly revised in 1993 to include rarities like 'Prowler' and 'Where Eagles Dare' among others). It sounds as thin and dry as its predecessor, being produced by Steve Harris on his own, and the mix exposes the lack of balancing guitar tones with both Dave Murray and Janick Gers play Fender Stratocasters through Marshalls.

Released on 18 October 1993, *A Real Dead One* would not only be the first Maiden album after Dickinson's exit the previous August, but it would also serve to remind the listener of what Maiden were now sorely lacking: Adrian Smith's guitar playing and backing vocals. The tracklisting of the album runs the gamut from a poor-sounding 'The Number of the Beast', via 'Sanctuary' in its first appearance on a proper international Maiden album release, to another poor-sounding classic with the penultimate track '2 Minutes to Midnight'. Album closer 'Hallowed Be Thy Name (live)' was chosen as the album's single, complete with cover art in which Dickinson is impaled on a Devil's Pitchfork by Eddie, and featured for its B-side 'Wasted Years (live)' (a post-1985 track not included on *A Real Live One* earlier in the year) and 'Wrathchild (live)' (which was left off *A Real Dead One* for no other apparent reason than the need for a B-side).

LIVE AT DONINGTON

Just three weeks after *A Real Dead One*, Harris and Maiden released their third (!) live album of 1993. *Live at Donington* (also released on video as *Donington Live 1992*) is the complete recording of Maiden's performance at the 1992 Monsters of Rock festival in Donington, England. Released on 8 November 1993 as limited-edition double CD and triple vinyl packages, *Live at Donington* was remastered as a regular CD and digital addition to the Maiden catalogue in 1998. Its greatest strength, relative to the two earlier 1993 live records, is the fact that it features a concert in its entirety, giving the listener ample room to admire the fired-up performances of Dickinson, Harris and McBrain in particular. Harris' production, however, is as sandpaper-dry and unpleasant on the ears as both the previous live albums. An interesting footnote to this recording is the appearance of Adrian Smith for the 'Running Free' encore, in what is Maiden's first performance with their future three-guitar line-up.

ROCK IN RIO

After a lack of live albums throughout the Blaze Bayley era in the mid to late 1990s, the few live B-sides to singles being discussed briefly in the book's part two, Iron Maiden and their live records returned with a vengeance at the dawn of the new millennium. With Bruce Dickinson and Adrian Smith re-joining Maiden in a three-guitar outfit that also retained Smith's replacement Janick Gers, the release of *Rock in Rio* on 25 March 2002 (accompanied by a concert video three months later) served to hammer home the point: Maiden were back.

Produced and mixed by Kevin Shirley, who had also helmed Maiden's 2000 studio album *Brave New World*, the miles of distance to the low-fi live albums of 1993 are overwhelmingly apparent as the band storm through 'The Wicker Man', 'Ghost of the Navigator' and 'Brave New World' to kick things off. Blending Bayley era gems 'Sign of the Cross' and 'The Clansman' into a set that otherwise plays it safe with classic material like 'The Trooper' and 'Hallowed Be Thy Name', this is Maiden working their way towards a new peak of performance and production quality. 'Run to the Hills (live in 2001)' was released as a part of several 'Run to the Hills' single formats in 2002, in financial support of former drummer Clive Burr's MS Trust Fund.

More interesting setlists and tour concepts would follow, but what Maiden and Shirley created here was nothing less than *Live After Death* for a new generation of fans, the live album to measure all others by. Now safely referred to as a classic, *Rock in Rio* (filmed and recorded at Maiden's headlining performance at the Brazil mega-festival in January 2001, the final show of their *Brave New World Tour*) consolidated Iron Maiden as a force to be reckoned with in hard rock music going forward, not simply looking back in nostalgia.

BBC ARCHIVES

On 4 November 2002 Iron Maiden released the box set *Eddie's Archive*, in which can be found three double-disc CD packages: *Best of the B-sides* (discussed in the next chapter as one of Maiden's compilation albums), *Beast over Hammersmith* (coming right up), and *BBC Archives*. The latter is a collection of live performances recorded by British broadcaster BBC Radio over the years from 1979 to 1988. Produced by the broadcaster's Tony Wilson, this is a real gem for fans of the band and music historians alike.

The journey documented herein begins on 14 November 1979, when Iron Maiden records a radio broadcast of the tracks 'Iron Maiden', 'Running Free', 'Transylvania' and 'Sanctuary'. The performance features guitarist Tony Parsons, who also appears on Maiden's two tracks on the 1980 *Metal for Muthas* compilation album, as well as early Maiden drummer Doug Sampson. Parsons and Sampson would shortly be replaced by Dennis Stratton and Clive Burr in time for the early 1980 recording of Iron Maiden's debut album. But this late 1979 performance is a rollicking example of how good Maiden had already become, aided by a full and clear sound recording courtesy of Wilson that arguably out-matches what Maiden would achieve with their debut album. Parsons must also be singled out for delivering a remarkably unique guitar solo in 'Sanctuary', only a few weeks of time separating him from being immortalised on the band's first proper record.

Next up are Maiden's two Reading Festival appearances on 23 August 1980 and 28 August 1982, as the band morphs through line-ups with guitarist Dennis Stratton and drummer Clive Burr into the coming of guitarist Adrian Smith and singer Bruce Dickinson. Dickinson's predecessor Paul Di'Anno is on absolutely blistering form in the 1980 recording, delivering career-high performances of tracks like 'Remember Tomorrow', while the sheer energy of the Dickinson-fronted Maiden in the 1982 recording from their *The Number of the Beast* world tour is astounding.

Capping the double-disc set is a partial presentation of Maiden's headlining appearance at the Donington *Monsters of Rock* festival on 20 August 1988. There must certainly exist a complete recording of this show, a further three tracks not included here were featured on the 'The Clairvoyant' single in late 1988, and hopefully Maiden will come around to issuing the complete concert in a special box set at some point. For now, there are plenty of highlights in this abridged *BBC Archives* edition of the concert, including a diabolical 'Moonchild' that opens the show and a mesmerizing 'Infinite Dreams' that showcases the diversity and strength of Maiden's material in the late 1980s.

BEAST OVER HAMMERSMITH

Produced by front-of-house engineer Doug Hall in conjunction with Steve Harris, *Beast over Hammersmith* was recorded at London's Hammersmith Odeon on 20 March 1982. This was so early in the 1982 tour that it was actually before the 22 March release of *The Number of the Beast*. Consequently, the listener is treated to the strange experience of hearing a complete hush in the audience as then-unknown tracks from the forthcoming album roll out.

This is Iron Maiden on the cusp of international success, before they knew that *The Number of The Beast* would be a worldwide smash hit. However, Maiden with Dickinson at the helm are already 100 percent convinced of their own power, bursting onto the stage with a glorious rendition of the *Killers* track 'Murders in The Rue Morgue'. Picking highlights from *Beast over Hammersmith* is a futile effort, every single song vying for the spot. But mention must be made of the definitive version of 'Children of the Damned' and awe-inspiring Dickinson performances of 'The Prisoner' and 'Hallowed Be Thy Name'. Even Di'Anno-era juggernauts like 'Phantom of the Opera' and 'Killers' are turned into Dickinson-era classics with effortless ease, anchored by a powerful Harris and Hall production.

Beast over Hammersmith was finally available in its entirety with the 4 November 2002 release of the *Eddie's Archive* box set, and it would also be released on heavyweight vinyl in a triple-LP package with the remastered *The Number of the Beast* in 2022, titled *The Number of the Beast over Hammersmith*. With the appearance of an abridged edit of the shelved concert film in the 2004 *The Early Days* DVD package, this pivotal and essential Iron Maiden recording has eventually found its several proper places in their catalogue.

DEATH ON THE ROAD

The second Iron Maiden live album with the reformed Smith and Dickinson line-up, once again produced and mixed by Kevin Shirley, was released on 29 August 2005. Recorded on a single night in Dortmund, Germany on the *Dance of Death* tour in late 2003, the album (and the accompanying concert

DVD) documents a Maiden show that upped the theatrics considerably and focused on key material from the most recent studio record. Although the *Dance of Death* album was admittedly an inconsistent collection of new Maiden tunes, the high points of the record are high indeed, as these live versions argue forcefully. The title track itself, 'Rainmaker', 'Paschendale' and 'Journeyman' receive outstanding renditions here, alongside the expected classics plus a very unexpected version of the Blaze Bayley era deep cut 'Lord of the Flies' from *The X Factor*. 'The Trooper (live in 2003)' was picked as the album's single, with a combination of live tracks (some rarities recorded on their 2005 *Early Days* summer tour) and the original 1983 recording spread over different formats.

Flight 666

The concept that really opened up Iron Maiden's commercial potential and ushered in the second golden age of their career was putting the entire band and crew, along with all their stage equipment, into a Boeing 757 piloted by Bruce Dickinson, and going around the globe on a world tour that recreated the classic *Powerslave* stage show. Their media profile and ticket sales shot through the roof on the 2008–09 tour, and the *Flight 666* album and documentary film was recorded and shot during a run of concerts in Asia, Australasia, North and South America and released on 22 May 2009. Once again produced by Kevin Shirley, who continues to bring punch and clarity to the Maiden sound, the album is a romp through much of Maiden's 1980s highlights, plus the ever present 'Fear of the Dark', including some career-high performances of 'Revelations', 'Powerslave' and 'Rime of the Ancient Mariner'. Unthinkable a decade earlier, times had truly changed.

En Vivo!

Following the pattern of the previous live album, *En Vivo!* was recorded and filmed in Santiago, Chile on the 2011 *The Final Frontier* tour. The tour had seen another globetrotting and Dickinson-piloted airplane outing, and the album and concert video were released as a commemoration on 26 March 2012. With a great Shirley production and the band on top form, what ultimately lets the album down is a much less interesting setlist than *Flight 666*, Maiden now focused on their most recent album plus a batch of predictable classics. The performance highlight is Dickinson's treatment of the new album's 'The Talisman'.

Maiden England '88

This is the live album that never was in the 1980s, but that would finally arrive on 25 March 2013. At the end of the *Seventh Son of a Seventh Son* tour in 1988, Iron Maiden filmed and recorded their two appearances in Birmingham, England for a concert video to follow up 1985's *Live After Death*. Live albums were much less common back then, and it would probably be seen as a bit too soon, but a live video was released in 1989. Produced by Martin Birch, the soundtrack to the live video would eventually be released on CD as an abridged version in 1994, alongside a reissue of the VHS video, but when Maiden started revisiting their history in the 2000s, they eventually arrived at *Maiden England* and paired the DVD reissue with a double CD and vinyl picture disc onslaught of the entire concert.

In retrospect, Iron Maiden could have released a trilogy of fantastic live albums in the 1980s: *Beast over Hammersmith* in 1982 (which was eventually released on CD in 2002 and double vinyl in 2022), *Live After Death* in 1985 (the classic era zenith of their early career), and then *Maiden England* in 1989. It was not to be back then, but it is very satisfying for fans to have them alongside each other at long last. The only thing missing to make the set complete is a proper heavyweight audiophile vinyl version of *Maiden England*.

The 1988 *Seventh Son of a Seventh Son* live set is a great companion to the 1985 *Powerslave* set that graces *Live After Death*, particularly the tour's final UK leg where rare gems like 'Killers' and 'Still Life' were added in place of more common fare like 'The Trooper'. The Birmingham recording thus shares precious few tracks with *Live After Death*, being focused on then recent material like 'Infinite Dreams' and 'Wasted Years', with a spellbinding 'Seventh Son of a Seventh Son' sitting comfortably in the epic seat that 'Rime of the Ancient Mariner' had previously made its own.

THE BOOK OF SOULS: LIVE CHAPTER

For some reason, Maiden and their management now sanctioned the dropping of the ever-reliable Kevin Shirley and let Steve Harris produce and mix their live albums henceforth himself, along with his protégé Tony Newton. An unsettling throwback to the direction of the 1993 live albums, *The Book of Souls: Live Chapter* sounds markedly less punchy and crisp than any of the live albums Shirley had mixed for them post-2000. Recorded across the world on the 2016–17 *The Book of Souls* tour, their triumphant return to the stage following singer Bruce Dickinson's successful cancer battle, it is modelled on *Flight 666* (including the fact that Maiden now flew with Bruce again, this time in a 747) but it sounds nowhere near as good. Released on 17 November 2017, the highlights here include the long-awaited return to a live album of the underplayed 'Children of the Damned', an unexpected but well-positioned 'Powerslave', and the title track 'The Book of Souls' from their current album.

NIGHTS OF THE DEAD, LEGACY OF THE BEAST: LIVE IN MEXICO CITY

If the previous live album had been fair enough, the Harris and Newton production makes this one an unpleasant listening experience. Which is all the harder to bear because the *Legacy of the Beast* tour in 2018–19 found Maiden frequently on top of their game and performing a set that included the *Piece of Mind* rarities 'Where Eagles Dare' and 'Flight of Icarus' (the latter had not been performed live since 1987!), alongside Blaze Bayley era highlights 'Sign of the Cross' and 'The Clansman', topped off with post-2000 gems 'The Wicker Man' and 'For the Greater Good of God'. It is hard to accept that we only get to hear this in a mix where Dickinson sounds like he is singing through a plastic tube and the audience ambience seems like some weird woosh of science fiction sound effects.

As the title says it was recorded in Mexico City, in September 2019, but a look around YouTube will reveal that the band, and Dickinson in particular, had turned in much finer performances many times earlier in the tour. Some would reasonably speculate that the relatively high sales rate of physical formats in Latin America is the reason for Maiden's regular focus on recordings from these shores. Released on 20 November 2020, it might after all have been a bit of a pandemic stopgap for Maiden in the year or two that they were forced off the road, but it still sounds painfully like a missed opportunity to create another classic live album that could have rivalled *Rock in Rio* and even *Live After Death*.

19

Compilations

BEST OF THE BEAST

On 23 September 1996 Iron Maiden finally released their first compilation album. The band had just completed their first album and tour cycle with new singer Blaze Bayley, 1995's *The X Factor*, and a compilation probably made sense as a way to engage fans until the next studio album would be ready. It made a little less sense, however, in the way that it effectively put the spotlight on how great Maiden once had been compared to what they now were. Just the year before, their record company had reissued the Maiden catalogue on CD with bonus discs, and just a couple of years later the catalogue would be remastered and reissued again. With *Best of the Beast* thrown in, this made it hard for the new Bayley line-up to escape the immense shadow of Maiden's past.

Best of the Beast was issued as a single CD, a double CD, and a 4-LP set, the latter being especially sought after as a collector's item. It is hard to argue with most of the classic material on hand, but equally hard to fathom the absence of the early Dickinson era highlight 'Children of the Damned', their biggest American radio song 'Flight of Icarus', their arguably best ever title track 'Powerslave', and the late 1980s masterpiece and British hit single 'Infinite Dreams', all four of them missing even from the 4-LP version with its gargantuan 34 tracks. The new song added to the collection, 'Virus', might have been good enough to make either *The X Factor* or *Virtual XI*, but in place of any of the missing songs it is something of an insult. As a slight compensation, the 4-LP version does include all four tracks from the legendary *The Soundhouse Tapes* sessions in late 1978.

Ed Hunter

In the summer of 1999 Iron Maiden were set to hit the road with the reformed line-up that welcomed back both Bruce Dickinson and Adrian Smith, and some sort of product to go along with the tour was called for. Their long-gestating computer game *Melt* had by this point been shelved and replaced by *Ed Hunter*, and it was decided to combine the game with a double CD compilation. As a novel approach to compiling the tracks, fans were invited to vote for their favourite songs through the Iron Maiden website.

Released on 17 May 1999, *Ed Hunter* presented a fair overview of Maiden's career and certainly primed audiences for the imminent return of Dickinson and Smith. Running the gamut from the early days of 'The Trooper' and its like, via late 1980s Smith masterpieces 'Wasted Years' and 'Stranger in a Strange Land', to recent Blaze Bayley tracks like 'Futureal', it might not be a hundred percent reflective of the fans' votes, but the collection is certainly comprehensive and less convoluted than *Best of the Beast*. The US version of the game and compilation also contained a hidden curiosity track where Dickinson had recorded new vocals on the original version of 'Wrathchild' from 1981's *Killers*.

Best of the B-sides

Iron Maiden have always taken pride in presenting good bonus material for fans who buy their singles. Back in the 1980s it was common for bands to simply issue an album track with another album track, but Maiden would often release live versions and non-album cover songs that made their singles more fun for fans and more worthwhile to collect. As part of the box set *Eddie's Archive*, released on 4 November 2002, Maiden issued a double CD collection titled *Best of the B-sides* that serves to provide much of this material without the need to collect every single.

Some standouts are missing, like 1982's 'Total Eclipse' (an original Maiden track) and 1988's 'Massacre' (a Thin Lizzy cover), but most of the collection's first disc is great material. The 1986 and 1988 recordings are of particularly high quality, like the pop-rock hooks of 'Reach Out', sung by Adrian Smith, or the ferocious energy of 'Prowler '88', a re-recording of the classic song from their first album. On the second disc can be found such rarities as a catchy *The X Factor* left-over called 'Justice of the Peace', which should undeniably have made the album, and 1999 live versions of 'Futureal' and 'Wasted Years' by the reformed later era line-up.

Edward the Great

On the same day that *Eddie's Archive* was released, 4 November 2002, Iron Maiden also issued yet another compilation CD, this time titled *Edward the Great* (as in Eddie, you all know). This release was clearly aimed at potential new fans, running through Maiden singles mostly from the Dickinson era in the 1980s, and it held no interest for anyone already familiar with the band.

THE ESSENTIAL IRON MAIDEN

This North American collection from Sony Music Entertainment's *The Essential* series, released on 12 July 2005, is another one of the obligatory collections that every major legacy artist seems to pile up in the later stages of their career. However, as Maiden collections after 2000 go, it is notable for including a rare representation of the Paul Di'Anno era. 'Phantom of the Opera', 'Wrathchild' and 'Killers' are all featured as original versions, and it would be Di'Anno's last appearance on a Maiden collection. The same goes for Blaze Bayley, who is heard here on 'Sign of the Cross', 'Man on the Edge', 'Futureal' and 'The Clansman' for the last time in an official Maiden collection.

SOMEWHERE BACK IN TIME: THE BEST OF 1980–1989

This collection was released on 12 May 2008, the fifth retrospective Iron Maiden compilation album in just twelve years. To coincide with the DVD reissue of *Live After Death*, and the start of their massive *Somewhere Back in Time* world tour with a modernised *Powerslave* stage set, Iron Maiden now reset their history representation by deleting Paul Di'Anno. It might be a fair argument that using only the current voice of the band (and let's face it, Bruce Dickinson is the best) is less confusing to much of their audience, but it's equally easy to argue that this removal is a cynical refashioning. A single CD collection, *Somewhere Back in Time* notably includes 'Children of the Damned' in such company for the first time, but for many fans it will always grate that all the Di'Anno era material is taken from *Live After Death* and thus performed by Dickinson.

FROM FEAR TO ETERNITY: THE BEST OF 1990–2010

On 6 June 2011 it was Blaze Bayley's turn to be erased from the Iron Maiden history representation. *Somewhere Back in Time* and the 2-CD *From Fear to Eternity* are now the only Iron Maiden compilations in print, and for the latter all of Bayley's performances are replaced by Bruce Dickinson live recordings. It is notable, however, that the days of singles are now past, with the collection including majestic album-only numbers like 'Brave New World', 'Blood Brothers', 'Paschendale' and 'For the Greater Good of God', proof indeed of Maiden's strong later-era output.

20

Video Albums

Iron Maiden were always at the forefront of creativity and commercialism with the video format. From the late 1980 promo video that went with their 'Women in Uniform' single, they would always provide a video counterpart to their singles throughout their career. The longform video, often labelled a video album, would also be a Maiden forte. All their releases of this kind, including documentaries and concert features, are summed up here.

LIVE AT THE RAINBOW
Comprising a half-hour of concert footage filmed at London's Rainbow Theatre in December 1980, *Live at the Rainbow* was Iron Maiden's first concert video, released on the VHS format in May 1981. The show is notable for being one of the band's earliest with guitarist Adrian Smith, and it features an early version of the song 'Killers' with work-in-progress lyrics. The band were about to commence recording of the *Killers* album that would be out in early 1981.

VIDEO PIECES
This is simply a collection of the promo videos that were made for the singles from *The Number of the Beast* in 1982 and *Piece of Mind* in 1983: 'Run to the Hills', 'The Number of the Beast', 'Flight of Icarus' and 'The Trooper'. It was released in the summer of 1983.

BEHIND THE IRON CURTAIN
Maiden opened their *Powerslave* tour in Eastern Europe in August 1984, on the other side of what was then referred to as the Communist Bloc's Iron Curtain. Touring in countries like Poland, Hungary and Yugoslavia was very uncommon for major American or Western European artists, and the

commotion and excitement of Iron Maiden coming to town is fascinatingly illustrated in this half-hour combination of documentary and concert footage released in late 1984. A one-hour expanded version with much more footage of Maiden on stage early in the *Powerslave* tour was included on the 2008 *Live After Death* DVD.

LIVE AFTER DEATH

Filmed at Long Beach Arena in Southern California in March 1985, as the *Powerslave* tour was at its peak, *Live After Death* is the ultimate classic Maiden concert film. With a blistering soundtrack produced and mixed by Martin Birch (and remixed into glorious surround by Kevin Shirley for the DVD version), even the fact that Bruce Dickinson is exhausted beyond managing the highest notes does not detract from the theatrical spectacle of pyramids and mummy Eddies. *Live After Death*, released on VHS in October 1985, would forever be the yardstick by which to measure a Maiden show from any era, and the 2008 DVD reissue with its accompanying 90-minute documentary about the *Powerslave* and *Live After Death* era is a must-have for fans and rock historians alike. Another nugget of gold therein is additional concert footage from the 1985 Rock in Rio festival in Brazil.

12 WASTED YEARS

The first Iron Maiden retrospective, *12 Wasted Years* was filmed and compiled during the *Somewhere in Time* cycle and looked back on the twelve years of Maiden's existence from the start in 1975 until 1987. Originally released on VHS in October 1987, the documentary was included in its entirety on the 2013 DVD reissue of *Maiden England*.

MAIDEN ENGLAND

A brilliant 1980s counterpart to *Live After Death*, this is a concert performance filmed and recorded in Birmingham, England at the end of the *Seventh Son of a Seventh Son* tour in November 1988. The setlist and stage production is very different from the *Powerslave* show captured for the *Live After Death* video, although the Martin Birch mix is sadly not as good. However, this was neatly rectified with the 2013 DVD reissue slightly retitled *Maiden England '88*, where Kevin Shirley's surround mix provided a fatter and crisper sound experience. The DVD also added the concert encore that was originally cut from the original VHS release in late 1989.

THE FIRST TEN YEARS: THE VIDEOS

This is a collection of every Iron Maiden promo video in the 1980 to 1990 period, up to and including the 'Holy Smoke' video. The collection was reissued in 1992 as *From There to Eternity*, featuring an additional five videos from the 1990 to 1992 period, and would also form the basis of the later DVD collection *Visions of the Beast*.

DONINGTON LIVE 1992

A strangely unaffecting and bewildering concert video, *Donington Live 1992* is bogged down both by its self-consciously artsy photography and editing (seemingly masterminded by director Samuel Bayer) as well as the fact that it arrived in the immediate aftermath of Bruce Dickinson leaving the band. The soundtrack mix by Steve Harris is unpleasant too. Originally released on VHS in late 1993, it was touted by manager Rod Smallwood many years ago as being in the pipeline for a DVD reissue, but it has understandably never appeared.

RAISING HELL

Another feature to be released in the immediate post-Dickinson era, *Raising Hell* is in fact his last performance with the band prior to his departure. The concept is a Maiden live concert alongside macabre performances by cheesy horror illusionist Simon Drake. The show was broadcast in late August 1993, making it a sort of coda to the *Fear of the Dark* cycle, and subsequently released on VHS worldwide and on DVD in the United States in 1994. Like the previous *Donington Live 1992* concert film, it has never since been reissued.

CLASSIC ALBUMS: THE NUMBER OF THE BEAST

After a dearth of video material in the Blaze Bayley period, Iron Maiden were about to speed up for the DVD age, fittingly kicking things off with a late 2001 retrospective look at one of their most successful and beloved albums. *Classic Albums: The Number of the Beast* is part of a British documentary series about, well, classic albums. It features great interviews with the band (including the rarely seen Clive Burr) and their producer Martin Birch about the making of a legendary Iron Maiden album.

ROCK IN RIO

The first Iron Maiden concert video to be produced specifically for DVD and the surround sound treatment, *Rock in Rio* was filmed in January 2001 and released in June 2002. It was edited by Steve Harris (which some fans are always unhappy about) and mixed by Kevin Shirley (which was a huge step up from the concert albums and videos of the 1990s). In Harris' favour, it must be noted that the original edit as delivered was a disaster, according to both Harris and Shirley. The Maiden chief and bassist then took it upon himself to spend six months locked in a room, editing from scratch the concert video that has by now become a latter-day classic for fans and critics alike.

VISIONS OF THE BEAST
This is essentially an updated DVD version of the earlier *The First Ten Years* video collection, adding promo videos from the 1993 to 2001 period. The 2-DVD release also features a series of alternative videos for selected songs where the footage is interspersed with animation scenes by the Camp Chaos animation studio.

THE EARLY DAYS
The first entry in Iron Maiden's series of DVD reissues and documentaries about their history, this late 2004 release served as the primer and foundation for the 2005 *Early Days* tour where the band performed material only from the first four Iron Maiden albums. Included here is amateur footage from London's Ruskin Arms pub in 1980, the *Live at the Rainbow* 1981 video, an abridged version of *Beast over Hammersmith* from 1982, and the shortened Dortmund festival set from the 1983 *Piece of Mind* tour. Best of all is the in-depth feature-length documentary 'The History of Iron Maiden: Part 1'. The subsequent parts 2 and 3 can be found on the *Live After Death* and *Maiden England* DVD reissues, respectively.

DEATH ON THE ROAD
A neat follow-up and companion to *Rock in Rio*, this Dortmund concert from late 2003 was brilliantly (even if some would say frantically) edited by Steve Harris and mixed by Kevin Shirley. Released in February 2006, it delivers the moodiest and most theatrical Iron Maiden concert film yet. Look no further for mesmerising versions of 'Paschendale' and 'Journeyman', among other highlights. The classic tracks in the set are by now too familiar, but the band's performances are top-notch across the board.

FLIGHT 666
A Banger Films production, *Flight 666* is a documentary film about the first leg of Iron Maiden's 2008 *Somewhere Back in Time* world tour, the part that saw them fly around the globe in an aeroplane called Ed Force One. The feature-length documentary itself is good, but the real treat with the DVD and Blu-ray release is the inclusion of the entire concert as shot throughout this early leg of the tour, with a great surround mix from Kevin Shirley. Released in May 2009, somehow the concert film manages the trick of feeling like one concert even if it is spread across continents song by song.

En Vivo!

Very much patterned on the previous *Flight 666* entry, *En Vivo!* was also filmed by Scot McFadyen and Sam Dunn's Banger Films, this time during the airplane leg of the 2011 *The Final Frontier* world tour. The *Behind the Beast* documentary that accompanies the concert on this DVD and Blu-ray release is not nearly as interesting as *Flight 666*, but once again the concert footage and its Kevin Shirley surround mix is superb. The feature was released on DVD and Blu-ray in March 2012, this seems to be the last time that Maiden would ever film a concert in a single city for an official release.

The Book of Souls: Live Chapter

Marking the end of an era in several ways, this concert video was never released on DVD or Blu-ray, and Maiden have not released anything in these formats since. Instead, *The Book of Souls: Live Chapter* was made available as a live stream and subsequently could be purchased as a digital download. The songs were filmed and recorded across the world on the 2016–17 tour in the fashion of the previous concert film *Flight 666*. This also marked the first time since *Rock in Rio* that Kevin Shirley was not on hand for the mix, being replaced here by the much less accomplished Tony Newton.

Since then, Iron Maiden have delivered three mind-blowing sets and productions that have raised the bar in terms of their live history. First, *Legacy of the Beast* in 2018–19, with its broad scope setlist and Spitfire-led massive production values, only to be commemorated with the mediocre *Nights of the Dead, Legacy of the Beast: Live in Mexico City* live album and no visual companion. Second, *The Future Past* in 2023–24, with the inspired combination of new album *Senjutsu* with underplayed classic *Somewhere in Time*, not celebrated with any kind of release. And in 2025 to 2026 Maiden are on the road with one of their most impressive setlists and stage productions of all time, taking onstage video technology to the next level, on their fiftieth anniversary *Run for Your Lives* tour. Maiden have announced that the Paris concert in 2026 will be filmed with a phone ban in effect, for a future concert feature. This should be a great celebration of Maiden's legacy and longevity.

Discography

Studio albums (see Parts One, Two & Three)

Iron Maiden	14 April 1980, EMI/Capitol
Killers	16 February 1981, EMI/Capitol
The Number of the Beast	22 March 1982, EMI/Capitol
Piece of Mind	16 May 1983, EMI/Capitol
Powerslave	3 September 1984, EMI/Capitol
Somewhere in Time	29 September 1986, EMI/Capitol
Seventh Son of a Seventh Son	11 April 1988, EMI/Capitol
No Prayer for the Dying	1 October 1990, EMI/Epic
Fear of the Dark	11 May 1992, EMI/Epic
The X Factor	2 October 1995, EMI/CMC
Virtual XI	23 March 1998, EMI/CMC
Brave New World	29 May 2000, EMI/Columbia
Dance of Death	8 September 2003, EMI/Columbia
A Matter of Life and Death	25 August 2006, EMI/Sanctuary
The Final Frontier	13 August 2010, EMI/UMe
The Book of Souls	4 September 2015, Parlophone/BMG
Senjutsu	3 September 2021, Parlophone/BMG

Live albums (see Part Four)

Live After Death	14 October 1985, EMI/Capitol
A Real Live One	22 March 1993, EMI/Capitol
A Real Dead One	18 October 1993, EMI/Capitol
Live at Donington	8 November 1993, EMI
Rock in Rio	25 March 2002, EMI/Columbia
BBC Archives	4 November 2002, EMI/Columbia/Sanctuary
Beast over Hammersmith	4 November 2002, EMI/Columbia/Sanctuary
Death on the Road	29 August 2005, EMI/Sanctuary
Flight 666	25 May 2009, EMI/UMe
En Vivo!	26 March 2012, EMI/UMe
Maiden England '88	25 March 2013, EMI/UMe
The Book of Souls: Live Chapter	17 November 2017, Parlophone/BMG
Nights of the Dead, Legacy of the Beast: Live in Mexico City	20 November 2020, Parlophone/BMG

Compilations (see Part Four)

Best of the Beast	23 September 1996, EMI/Castle
Ed Hunter	17 May 1999, EMI/Columbia
Best of the B-sides	4 November 2002, EMI/Columbia/Sanctuary
Edward the Great	4 November 2002, EMI/Columbia
The Essential Iron Maiden	12 July 2005, Sanctuary
Somewhere Back in Time: The Best of 1980-1989	12 May 2008, EMI/UMe
From Fear to Eternity: The Best of 1990–2010	6 June 2011, EMI/UMe

Singles and EPs (see Parts One, Two, Three & Four)

The Soundhouse Tapes	9 November 1979, Rock Hard
'Running Free'	8 February 1980, EMI
'Sanctuary'	23 May 1980, EMI
'Women in Uniform'	27 October 1980, EMI
'Live!! +one'	December 1980, EMI
'Twilight Zone'	2 March 1981, EMI
'Purgatory'	15 June 1981, EMI
'Maiden Japan'	14 September 1981, EMI/Capitol
'Run to the Hills'	12 February 1982, EMI/Capitol
	Reissued: 11 March 2002
'The Number of the Beast'	26 April 1982, EMI/Capitol
	Reissued: 3 January 2005
'Flight of Icarus'	11 April 1983, EMI/Capitol
'The Trooper'	20 June 1983, EMI/Capitol
	Reissued: 15 August 2005
'2 Minutes to Midnight'	6 August 1984, EMI/Capitol
'Aces High'	22 October 1984, EMI/Capitol
'Running Free (live)'	23 September 1985, EMI/Capitol
'Run to the Hills (live)'	2 December 1985, EMI/Capitol
'Wasted Years'	6 September 1986, EMI/Capitol
'Stranger in a Strange Land'	22 November 1986, EMI/Capitol
'Can I Play with Madness'	20 March 1988, EMI/Capitol
'The Evil That Men Do'	1 August 1988, EMI/Capitol
'The Clairvoyant'	7 November 1988, EMI
'Infinite Dreams (live)'	6 November 1989, EMI
'Holy Smoke'	10 September 1990, EMI/Epic
'Bring Your Daughter … to the Slaughter'	24 December 1990, EMI/Epic
'Be Quick or Be Dead'	13 April 1992, EMI/Epic
'From Here to Eternity'	29 June 1992, EMI/Epic
'Wasting Love'	1 September 1992, EMI
'Fear of the Dark (live)'	1 March 1993, EMI
'Hallowed Be Thy Name (live)'	4 October 1993, EMI

'Man on the Edge'	25 September 1995, EMI/CMC
'Lord of the Flies'	2 February 1996, EMI/CMC
'Virus'	2 September 1996, EMI
'The Angel and the Gambler'	9 March 1998, EMI/CMC
'Futureal'	28 July 1998, EMI/BMG
'The Wicker Man'	8 May 2000, EMI/Columbia
'Out of the Silent Planet'	23 October 2000, EMI/Columbia
'Run to the Hills (live in 2001)'	11 March 2002, EMI
'Wildest Dreams'	1 September 2003, EMI/Columbia
'Rainmaker'	24 November 2003, EMI
'No More Lies'	29 March 2004, EMI
'The Trooper (live in 2003)'	15 August 2005, EMI/Sanctuary
'The Reincarnation of Benjamin Breeg'	14 August 2006, EMI/Sanctuary
'Different World'	14 November 2006, EMI/Sanctuary
'El Dorado'	8 June 2010, digital
'Satellite 15 … The Final Frontier'	13 July 2010, video and promo
'Coming Home'	27 October 2010, promo
'Speed of Light'	14 August 2015, video and digital
'Empire of the Clouds'	16 April 2016, Parlophone
'The Writing on the Wall'	15 July 2021, video and digital
'Stratego'	19 August 2021, video and digital

Video albums (see Part Four)

Live at the Rainbow	May 1981, PMI
Video Pieces	July 1983, PMI
Behind the Iron Curtain	October 1984, PMI
Live After Death	23 October 1985, PMI
	DVD reissue: 4 February 2008, EMI
12 Wasted Years	October 1987, PMI
Maiden England	8 November 1989, PMI
	DVD reissue: 25 March 2013, EMI
The First Ten Years: The Videos	November 1990, PMI

Donington Live 1992	8 November 1993, PMI
Raising Hell	5 September 1994, PMI/BMG
Classic Albums: The Number of the Beast	26 November 2001, Eagle Vision
Rock in Rio	10 June 2002, Sanctuary
Visions of the Beast	2 June 2003, EMI
The Early Days	8 November 2004, EMI
Death on the Road	6 February 2006, EMI
Flight 666	21 April 2009, EMI
En Vivo!	26 March 2012, EMI
The Book of Souls: Live Chapter	17 November 2017, Parlophone

Sources

Daniels, Neil (2014). *Killers. The Origins of Iron Maiden: 1975–1983*. London: Soundcheck Books.
Dickinson, Bruce (2017). *What Does This Button Do? An Autobiography*. London: HarperCollins.
Everley, Dave (ed.) (2019). *Classic Rock* Platinum Series and *Metal Hammer* Present: *Iron Maiden – The Complete Story*. Future issue 05.
Henrik & Mattias (1996). 'A Conversation with Bruce Dickinson: Stockholm, Sunday April 28, 1996': http://www.bookofhours.net/beta/inter_960428.htm
Ling, Dave (2001). 'Face-off with Bruce Dickinson', in *Classic Rock* no. 33.
Marshall, Clay (2000). 'Interview with Bruce Dickinson, March 2000': https://web.archive.org/web/20141217150623/http:/maidenfans.com/index.php?ACT=module&name=rwarticles&show=59
O'Neill, Eamon (2020). Adrian Smith interview with eonmusic.com, August 2020: https://www.eonmusic.co.uk/adrian-smith-iron-maiden-eonmusic-interview-august-2020.html
Ott, Markus (ed.) (1990). *Metal Attack. Metal Hammer Special*, no. 5/90.
Paterson, Lawrence (2010). *At the End of the Day: The Story of the Blaze Bayley Band*. London: Metalbox Recordings Ltd.
Smith, Adrian (2020). *Monsters of River and Rock. My Life as Iron Maiden's Compulsive Angler*. London: Virgin Books.
Wall, Mick (1990). 'Portuguese Maiden O'War', in *Kerrang!* no. 306.
Wall, Mick (1990). 'Prayer Meeting', in *Kerrang!* no. 307.
Wall, Mick ([1998] 2004). *Run to the Hills. The Authorised Biography*. London: Sanctuary Publishing Limited.

See also www.maidenrevelations.com for further articles from the author on the history and aesthetics of Iron Maiden.